Chapter 1 - Security

Fundamentals

The Information Security Cycle

What is Information Security?

Information security refers to the protection of available information or information resources from unauthorized access, attacks, thefts or data damage.

What to Protect

Data – you need to protect data from getting corrupt or from being accessed without authorization

Resources – A physical resource is any device connected directly to a computer system and a Virtual resource refers to types of files, memory locations or network connections.

Collateral Damage

If the security of an organization's data and resources is compromised it may lead to a compromised reputation, loss of goodwill, reduced investor confidence, loss of customers and various financial losses.

Goals of Security

Prevention – Preventing users from gaining unauthorized access to confidential information should be the number one priority of information security professionals.

Detection – Detection occurs when a user is discovered trying to access unauthorized data or after information has been lost.

Recovery – When system data is compromised or damaged in a disaster or intrusion by unauthorized users, you may employ a process to recover vital data from the crashed system or data storage devices.

Risk

Risk is a concept that indicates exposure to the chance of damage or loss. It signifies the likelihood of a hazard or dangerous threat occurring.

Threats

A **threat** is any event or action that could potentially cause damage to an asset.

Vulnerabilities

A **vulnerability** is any condition that leaves a system open to harm.

Intrusions

An **intrusion** occurs when an attacker accesses a computer system without the authorization to do so.

- Physical intrusions
- Host-based intrusions

- Network-based intrusions

Attacks

An attack is a technique used to exploit a vulnerability in any application or physical computer system without the authorization to do so.

- Physical security attack
- Network based attacks, including wireless networks
- Software-based attacks
- Social engineering attacks
- Web application-based attacks

Controls

Controls are countermeasures that you need to put in place to avoid, mitigate or counteract security risks due to threats or attacks.

Types of Controls

Prevention controls – These help to prevent a threat or attack from exposing a vulnerability in the computer system.

Detection Controls – These help to discover if a threat or vulnerability has entered into the computer system.

Correction Controls – These help to mitigate the consequences of a threat or attack from adversely affecting the computer system.

The Security Management Process

Identify Security Controls – This involves detecting problems and determining how best to protect a system.

Implement Security Controls – This involves installing control mechanisms to prevent problems in a system.

Monitor Security Controls – This involves detecting and solving any security issues that arise after security controls are implemented.

Information Security Controls

The CIA Triad

Confidentiality – This is the fundamental principle of keeping information and communications private and protecting them from unauthorized access.

Integrity – This is the fundamental principle of keeping organization information accurate, free of errors and without unauthorized modifications.

Availability- This is the fundamental principle of ensuring that systems operate continuously and that authorized persons can access the data that they need.

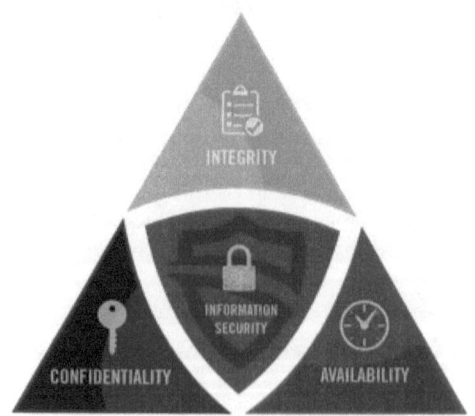

Non-repudiation

Non-repudiation is the goal of ensuring that the party that sent a transmission or created data remains associated with that data and cannot deny sending or creating that data.

Identification

Identification is a method that ensures that an entity requesting access to resources by using a certain set of credentials is the true owner of the credentials.

Authentication

Authentication is a method of validating a particular entity or individual's unique credentials.

Authentication Factors

Something you are, including physical characteristics, such as fingerprints or a retina pattern.

Something you have, such as a token or access card.

Something you know, such as a password.

Somewhere you are or are not, such as an approved IP address or GPS location.

Something you do, such as established keystroke patterns or tracing over a Windows 8.1 picture password.

Something you have   **Something you are**   **Something you know**

Authorization

Authorization is the process of determining what rights and privileges a particular entity has.

Access Control

Access control is the process of determining and assigning privileges to various resources, objects or data.

Access Control Methods

Mandatory Access Control (MAC) – In this model, access is controlled by comparing an object's security designation and a user's security clearance.

Discretionary Access Control (DAC) – In this model, access to each object is controlled on a customized basis, which is based on a user's identity.

Role-Based Access Control (RBAC) – In this model, users are assigned to predefined roles and network objects are configured to allow access only to specific roles.

Rule-Based Access Control – This is a non-discretionary technique that is based on a set of operational rules or restrictions.

Accounting and Auditing

Accounting is the process of tracking and recording system activities and resource access.

Auditing is the part of accounting in which a security professional examines logs of what was recorded.

Common Security Practices

Common security practices help implement access controls in ways that provide effective measures for the protection of data and resources.

- Implicit Deny
- Least Privilege
- Separation of Duties
- Job Rotation
- Mandatory vacation
- Time of day restrictions
- Privilege Management

Implicit Deny

The principle of implicit deny dictates that everything that is not explicitly allowed is denied.

Least Privilege

The principle of least privilege dictates that users and software should only have the minimal level of access that is necessary for them to perform the duties required of them.

Privilege Bracketing

The term privilege bracketing is used when privileges are given out only when needed, then revoked as soon as the task is finished or the need has passed.

Separation of Duties

Separation of duties states that no one person should have too much power or responsibility.

Job Rotation

The idea of job rotation is that no one person stays in a vital job role for too long.

Mandatory vacation

From a security standpoint, mandatory vacations provide an opportunity to review employees' activities.

Time of Day Restrictions

Time of day restrictions are controls that restrict the periods of time when users are allowed to access systems, which can be set using a group policy.

Orphaned Accounts

Orphaned accounts are user accounts that remain active even after the employees have left the organization.

Privilege Management

Privilege management is the use of authentication and authorization mechanisms to provide centralized or decentralized administration of user and group access control.

Privilege Management Infrastructure (PMI)

PMI is used to issue specific permissions and rights to users within the infrastructure.

Authentication Methods

Strong authentication is the first line of defense in the battle to secure network resources.

User Name / Password Authentication

In this type of authentication a user's username and password are compared against credentials stored in a database. If they match, the user is authenticated, otherwise is denied.

Tokens

Tokens are physical or virtual objects, such as smart cards, ID badges or data packets that store authentication information.

Smart Cards

A smart card is a plastic card containing an embedded computer chip that can store different types of electronic information. They are an example of token-based authentication.

Biometrics

Biometrics are authentication schemes based on the identification of individuals by their physical characteristics. This can involve a fingerprint scanner, a retinal scanner, a hand geometry scanner or voice-recognition and facial-recognition software.

Geolocation

Users who are attempting to authenticate from an approved location can be granted network access, while users who are trying to authenticate from a location that is not approved can be denied network access.

Keystroke Authentication

Keystroke authentication is a type of authentication that relies on detailed information that describes exactly when a keyboard key is pressed and released as someone types information into a computer or other electronic device.

Multi-factor Authentication

Multi-factor authentication is any authentication scheme that requires validation of two or more authentication factors. It can be a combination of who you are, what you have, what you know, where you are or are not and what you do.

Mutual Authentication

Mutual authentication is a security mechanism that requires that each party in a communication verifies each other's identity.

Cryptography Fundamentals

Cryptography is a powerful and complex weapon in the fight to maintain computer security.

Cryptography

Cryptography is the science of hiding information.

Use of Proven Technologies

The technologies and techniques used in cryptography should have a well-documented history of investigation by industry professionals.

Encryption and Decryption

Encryption is a cryptographic technique that converts data from plaintext or cleartext form into coded or ciphertext form.

Decryption is the companion technique that converts ciphertext back to cleartext.

Quantum Cryptography

Quantum cryptography is an experimental method of data encryption based upon quantum communication and computation.

A qubit is a unit of data that is encrypted by entangling data with a photon or electron that has a particular spin cycle which can be read using a polarization filter that controls spin.

If a qubit is read with an incorrect polarization filter, then it becomes unreadable and the receiver will know that someone may actually be eavesdropping.

Ciphers

A cipher is an algorithm used to encrypt or decrypt data.

A Simple Encryption Algorithm

A letter-substitution cipher, in which each letter of the alphabet is systematically replaced by another letter.

Cipher Types

Stream Cipher – A type of encryption that encrypts data one bit at a time.

Block Cipher – The cipher encrypts data one block at a time, often in 64-bit blocks. Some common modes of block cipher encryption are:

- Electronic Code Block (ECB) encryption
- Cipher block Chaining (CBC) encryption
- Propagating or Plaintext Cipher Block Chaining (PCBC) encryption
- Cipher Feedback mode (CFB) encryption
- Output Feedback mode (OFB) encryption
- Counter mode (CTR) encryption

Encryption and Security Goals

- Enables confidentiality
- Supports integrity
- Supports non-repudiation
- Protects passwords
- Used in access control mechanisms

Steganography

Steganography is an alternative cipher process that hides information by enclosing it in another file such as a graphic, movie or sound file.

Keys

An encryption key is a specific piece of information that is used in conjunction with an algorithm to perform encryption and decryption.

Keys can be static or ephemeral. Static keys are intended to be used for a relatively long time and for many instances within a key-establishment process, while ephemeral keys are generated for each individual communication segment or session.

One-Time Pad

The one-time pad is an encryption algorithm that was developed under the assumption that if a key was used once, was completely random and was kept totally secret, then it constituted the perfect method of encryption.

A Simple Encryption Key

In a simple letter-substitution algorithm, the key might be "replace each letter with the letter that is two letters following it in the alphabet."

Hashing Encryption

Hashing encryption is one-way encryption that transforms cleartext into ciphertext that is not intended to be decrypted. The result of the hashing process is called a hash, hash value or message digest.

Hashing Applications

- Password authentication schemes
- Hash value supports data integrity and non-repudiation
- File integrity verification during transfers

Hashing Encryption Algorithms

Message Digest 5 (MD5)

This algorithm produces a 128-bit message digest. It was created by Ronald Rivest but no longer considered a strong hash function.

Secure Hash Algorithm (SHA)

Modeled after MD5. E.g. SHA-160, SHA-256, SHA-384, SHA-512.

NT LAN Manager (NTLM#)

NTLMv1 and NTLMv2 are authentication protocols created by Microsoft®.

RACE Integrity Primitives Evaluation Message Digest (RIPEMD)

Based on design principles used in MD4. E.g. RIPEMD-128, RIPEMD-160, RIPEMD-256 and RIPEMD-320.

Hash-based Message Authentication Code (HMAC)

This is a method used to verify both the integrity and authenticity of a message by combining cryptographic hash functions, such as MD5 or SHA-1, with a secret key. E.g. HMAC-SHA1.

Symmetric Encryption

Symmetric encryption is a two-way encryption scheme in which encryption and decryption are both performed by the same key.

Symmetric Encryption Algorithms

Data Encryption Standard (DES)

A block-cipher symmetric encryption algorithm that encrypts data in 64-bit blocks using a 56-bit key with 8 bits used for parity.

Triple DES (3DES)

A symmetric encryption algorithm that encrypts data by processing each block of data three times using a different key each time.

Advanced Encryption Standard (AES)

A symmetric 128-, 192, or 256-bit block cipher called Rijndael after its creators, Joan Daemen and Vincent Rijmen meant to replace DES.

Blowfish

A freely available 64-bit block cipher algorithm that uses a variable key length. It was developed by Bruce Schneier.

Twofish

A symmetric key block cipher, similar to Blowfish, consisting of a block size of 128 bits and key sizes up to 256 bits.

Rivest Cipher (RC) 4, 5 and 6

A series of algorithms developed by Ronald Rivest. All have variable key lengths. RC4 is a stream cipher. RC5 and RC6 are variable-size block ciphers.

Asymmetric Encryption

Private Key

The private key is kept secret by one party during two-way encryption.

Public Key

The public key is given to anyone.

Key Generation

Key generation is the process of generating a public and private key pair by using a specific application.

Asymmetric Encryption Techniques

Rivest Shamir Adelman (RSA)

Named after its designers Ronald Rivest, Adi Shamir and Leonard Adelman, RSA was the first successful algorithm for public key encryption. It has variable key length and block size.

Diffie-Hellman (DH)

A cryptographic technique that provides for secure key exchange.

Elliptic curve cryptography (ECC)

Leverages the algebraic structures of elliptic curves over finite fields. ECC is used with wireless and mobile devices.

Diffie-Hellman Ephemeral (DHE)

A variant of DH that uses ephemeral keys to provide secure key exchange.

Elliptic Curve Diffie-Hellman Ephemeral (ECDHE)

A variant of DH that incorporates the use of ECC and ephemeral keys.

Key Exchange

Key exchange Is any method by which cryptographic keys are transferred among users, thus enabling the use of a cryptographic algorithm.

Digital Signatures

A digital signature is a message digest that has been encrypted again with a user's private key. Asymmetric encryption algorithms can be used with hashing algorithms to create digital signatures.

Encryption of the Hash

A digital signature is a hash that is then itself encrypted.

Cipher Suites

A cipher suite is a collection of symmetric and asymmetric encryption algorithms that are used to establish a secure connection between hosts.

Key exchange algorithm

Determines if and how the client and server will authenticate during the TLS connection handshake.

Bulk encryption algorithm

Encrypts the actual message stream and includes the key size.

Message authentication code algorithm

Creates the message digest.

Pseudorandom function

Creates the master secret, which is a 48-byte secret that is shared between the two systems being connected.

Session Keys

A session key is a single-use symmetric key that is used for encrypting all messages in a single series of related communications.

Perfect forward secrecy

Perfect forward secrecy is a property of public key cryptographic systems that ensures that any session key derived from a set of long-term keys cannot be compromised if one of the keys is compromised at a future date.

Key stretching

Key stretching is a technique that strengthens potentially weak cryptographic keys, such as passwords or passphrases created by people, against brute force attacks.

Password-Based Key Derivation Function 2 (PBKDF2)

This key derivation function uses five input parameters to create a derived key.

Bcrypt

Bcrypt is a key-derivation function based on the Blowfish cipher.

Security Policy fundamentals

Security Policies

A security policy is a formalized statement that defines how security will be implemented within a particular organization.

Need to Know

A security policy should specify who should have access to privileged information and on what basis.

Security Policy Components

Policy statement

Outlines the plan for the individual security component.

Standards

Define how to measure the level of adherence to the policy.

Guidelines

Suggestions, recommendations or best practices for how to meet the policy standard.

Procedures

Step-by-step instructions that detail how to implement components of the policy.

Common Security Policy Types

Acceptable use policy (AUP)

States the limits and guidelines that are set for users and others to make use of an organization's physical and intellectual resources.

Privacy policy

Defines standards for divulging organizational or personal information to other parties.

Audit policy

Details the requirements and parameters for risk assessment and audits of the organization's information and resources.

Extranet policy

Sets the requirements for third-party entries that desire access to an organization's networks.

Password policy

Defines standards for creating password complexity.

Wireless standards policy

Defines which wireless device can connect to an organization's network and how to use them in a safe manner that protects the organization's security.

Social media policy

Defines how the organization and its employees use social media such as blogs, Facebook, Twitter, LinkedIn etc.

Security Policy Standards Organizations

The SysAdmin, Audit, Networking and Security (SANS) Institute has identified a list of standard policy types and policy templates.

The Internet Engineering Task Force (IETF) provides templates such as Request for comments (RFC) 2196 for different security policies.

Group Policy

Windows security policies are configuration settings within the Microsoft® Windows® operating systems that control the overall security behavior of the system.

A **group policy** is a centralized account management feature available for Active Directory® on Windows Server systems.

Security Document Categories

System architecture

Physical documentation about the setup and configuration of your network and systems must be stored securely.

Change documentation

Changes in the configuration of data, systems and services are often tracked and documented to provide an official record of the correct current configuration.

Logs

System logs, especially those generated by the auditing security function, need to be protected from unauthorized access or tampering.

Inventories

Equipment and asset inventories provide a valuable source of information for attackers, whether they plan to mount an electronic attack against the system or resort to physical damage or theft.

Change Management

Change management is a systematic way of approving and executing change in order to assure maximum security, stability and availability of information technology services.

Document Handling Measures

Classification

The classification of a document not only determines who has the right to see or alter the document, but also the correct procedure for storing, archiving and handling the document.

Retention and storage

You policy should include standards and guidelines for how long different types of documents are retained to meet legal or policy requirements.

Disposal and destruction

There should be a plan for disposal or destruction of outdated documents.

Chapter 2 – Identifying

Security Threats and

Vulnerabilities

Social Engineering

Social Engineering Attacks

A social engineering attack is a type of attack that uses deception and trickery to convince unsuspecting users to provide sensitive data or to violate security guidelines.

Social Engineering Attack Scenarios

- An attacker creates an executable program file that prompts a network user for their user name and password and then records whatever the user inputs.
- An attacker contacts the help desk pretending to be a remote sales representative who needs assistance setting up his dial-in access.

- An attacker sends an executable file disguised as an electronic greeting card (e-card) or as a patch for an operating system or a specific application.

Social Engineering Targets

Social engineering typically takes advantage of users who are not technically knowledgeable, but it can also be directed against technical support staff if the attacker pretends to be a user who needs help.

Effectiveness

Social engineering is one of the most common and successful malicious techniques in information security. Because it exploits basic human trust, social engineering has proven to be a particularly effective way of manipulating people into misplacing this trust.

Types of Social Engineering

Spoofing

This is a human-based or software-based attack where the goal is to pretend to be someone else for the purpose of identity concealment.

Impersonation

This is a human-based attack where an attacker pretends to be someone they are not. A common scenario is when the attacker calls an employee and pretends to be calling from the help desk.

Hoax

This is an email-based or web-based attack that is intended to trick the user into performing undesired actions, such as deleting important system files in an attempt to remove a virus.

Phishing

Thi is a common type of email-based social engineering attack. In a phishing attack, the attacker sends an email that seems to come from a respected bank or other financial institution.

When attackers target a specific individual or institution, this social engineering technique is known as spear phishing. An attack similar to phishing called pharming, can be done by redirecting a request for a website, typically an e-commerce site, to a similar-looking, but fake, website.

Vishing

This is a human-based attack where the goal is to extract personal, financial or confidential information from the victim by using services such as the telephone system and IP-based voice messaging services (Voice over Internet Protocol [VoIP]) as the communication medium. This is also called voice phishing.

Whaling

This is a form of spear phishing that targets individuals or organizations that are known to possess a good deal of wealth.

URL hijacking

Also called typo squatting, this is the tactic of exploiting typos that users sometimes make when entering a URL into a browser.

Spam and spim

Spam is an email-based threat where the user's inbox is flooded with emails which acts as vehicles that carry advertising material for products or promotions for get-rich-quick schemes and can sometimes deliver viruses or malware.

Spim is an attack similar to spam that is propagated through instant messaging (IM) instead of through email.

Shoulder surfing

This is an attack where the goal is to look over the shoulder of an individual as he or she enters password information or PIN. This is very easy to do today with camera –equipped mobile phones.

Dumpster diving

This is an attack where the goal is to reclaim important information by inspecting the contents of trash containers.

Tailgating

Also known as piggy backing, this is a human-based attack where the attacker will slip in through a secure area following a legitimate employee.

VoIP

VoIP is a technology that enables you to deliver telephony information over IP networks.

Hackers and Attackers

Hackers and attackers are related terms for individuals who have the skills to gain access to computer systems through unauthorized or unapproved means.

Originally, hacker was a neutral term for a user who excelled at computer programming and computer system administration.

Attacker is a term that always represents a malicious system intruder.

White Hats and Black Hats

A white hat is a hacker who discovers and exposes security flaws in applications and operating systems so that manufacturers can fix them before they become widespread problems.

A black hat is a hacker who discovers and exposes security vulnerabilities for financial gain or for some malicious purpose.

Some who consider themselves white hats also discover and publicize security problems, but without the organization's knowledge or permission. They consider themselves to be acting for the common good. The hackers are commonly referred to as grey hats because of their moral ambiguity.

Categories of Attackers

Malicious insider (employees and contractors)

A malicious insider threat is a threat originating from an employee in an organization who performs malicious acts such as deleting critical information or sharing this critical information with outsiders, which may result in a certain amount of losses to the organization.

Electronic activist ("hacktivist")

The hacktivist is motivated by a desire to cause social change and might be trying to get media attention by disrupting services or promoting a message by replacing the information on public websites.

Data thief

This kind of attacker blatantly steals resources or confidential information for personal or financial gain.

Script kiddie

The novice attacker, known as a script kiddie, has limited technical knowledge and is motivated by a desire to gain and display technical skills.

Electronic vandal

This attacker simply wants to cause as much damage as possible, without any particular target or goal.

Cyberterrorist

This type of attacker tries to disrupt computer systems in an attempt to spread fear and panic.

Malware

Malware is not a monolithic threat but rather a collection of different methods that can exploit the vulnerabilities in your information security.

Malicious Code Attacks

A malicious code attack is a type of software attack where an attacker inserts some type of undesired or unauthorized software or malware into a target system.

Evidence of a Malicious Code attack

Malicious code is often combined with social engineering to convince a user that the malware is from a trusted or benign source.

Viruses

A virus is a piece of code that spreads from one computer to another by attaching itself to other files through a process of self-replication.

Worms

In computing, a worm is malware that, like a virus, replicates itself across the infected system.

Adware

Adware is software that automatically displays or downloads unsolicited advertisements when it is used.

Spyware

Spyware is surreptitiously installed malicious software that is intended to track and report the usage of target system or collect other data the author wishes to obtain.

Trojan Horses

Trojan horse, often simply called a Trojan is hidden malware that causes damage to a system or gives an attacker a platform for monitoring and/or controlling a system.

Rootkits

A rootkit is code that is intended to take full or partial control of a system at the lowest levels.

Logic Bombs

A logic bomb is a piece of code that sits dormant on a target computer until it is triggered by a specific event, such as a specific date.

Botnets

A botnet is a set of computers that has been infected by a control program called a bot that enables attackers to collectively exploit those computers to mount attacks. These infected machines are called zombies or drones.

Ransomware

Ransomware is an increasingly popular variety of malware in which an attacker infects a victim's computer with code that restricts the victim's access to their computer or the data on it.

Examples of Ransomware

Reveton: Reveton spread in 2012. Once it infected a computer, its payload would open windows on the target's computer that claimed the target had committed various computer crimes such as downloading pirated software.

CryptoLocker: CryptoLocker emerged in 2013. Once it infected a system, it would begin encrypting every storage device attached to that system.

Polymorphic Malware

Polymorphic malware is an encrypted virus that infects files with an encrypted copy of itself. A cryptographic key and decryption module is stored in plaintext with it. The decryption module is altered each time a virus infects a file making it very difficult for antivirus software to detect an infection that is constantly changing.

Armored Viruses

The defining quality of **armored viruses** is that they attempt to trick or shield themselves from antivirus software and security professionals. They contain obfuscated code to make it more difficult for security researchers to properly assess and reverse engineer them.

Software-Based Threats

Software Attacks

A **software attack** is any attack against software resources, including operating systems, applications, protocols and files.

Software Attack Combinations

A software attack might be used by itself or in combination with another type of attack such as a social engineering attack.

Password Attacks

A password attack is any type of attack in which the attacker attempts to obtain and make use of passwords illegitimately. The attacker can guess or steal passwords or crack encrypted password files.

Protecting Password Databases

Attackers know the storage locations of encrypted passwords on common systems such as the Security Accounts Manager (SAM) database on standalone Windows® systems.

Types of Password Attacks

Guessing

The simplest type of password attack is making individual, repeated attempts to guess a password by entering different common password values such as the user's name, spouse's name or a significant date.

Stealing

Passwords can be stolen by various means, including sniffing network communications, reading handwritten password notes or observing a user in the act of entering a password.

Dictionary attack

This attack type automates password guessing by comparing passwords against a predetermined list of possible password values, like words in a dictionary.

Brute force attack

The attacker uses a password-cracking software to attempt every possible alphanumeric password combination.

Rainbow tables

These are sets of related plaintext passwords and their hashers. The underlying principle of rainbow tables is to do the central processing unit (CPU) intensive work of generating hashes in advance, trading time saved during the attack for the disk space to store the tables.

Hybrid password attack

This attack type utilizes multiple attack methods, including dictionary, rainbow table and brute force attacks when trying to crack a password.

Birthday attack

This attack type exploits weaknesses in the mathematical algorithms used to generate hashes. This attack takes advantage of the probability of different inputs producing the same encrypted outputs, given a large enough set of inputs.

It is named after the surprising statistical fact that there is a 50 percent chance that two people in a group of 23 will share a birthday.

Password-Cracking Utilities

Commonly available password-cracking utilities include Ophcrack, LophtCrack, John the Ripper, Cain & Abel, THC Hydra, RainbowCrack, Aircrack, Airsnort, Pwdump, KerbCrack and Brutus.

Backdoor Attacks

A backdoor attack is a type of software attack where an attacker creates a software mechanism called a backdoor to gain access to a computer. The backdoor can be a software utility or an illegitimate user account.

Takeover Attacks

Backdoor attacks can be the first step in a takeover attack, in which the attacker assumes complete control over a system. A takeover attack will manifest itself in the loss of local control over the system under attack.

Application Attacks

Application attacks are software attacks that are targeted at web-based and other client-server applications. Those that specifically exploit the trust between a user and a server are called client-side attacks.

Types of application attacks

Cross-site scripting (XSS)

An attack that is directed toward sites with dynamic content. This is done by introducing malicious scripts into a trusted website.

Similarly, in a watering hole attack, an attacker targets specific groups or organizations, discovers which websites they frequent and injects malicious code into those sites.

Command injection attacks

- **SQL injection** is an attack that injects a Structured Query Language (SQL) query into the input data intended for the server by accessing the client side of the application. The query typically exploits and reads data in the database, modifies data in the database or executes administrative operations such as shutting down or recovering content off the database.

- **LDAP injection** is an attack that targets web-based applications by fabricating Lightweight Directory Access Protocol (LDAP) statements that are typically created from the user input. A system is vulnerable to this attack if it fails to filter user input properly.

- **XML injection** is an attack that injects corrupted eXtensible Markup Language (XML) query data so that an attacker can again access to the XML data structure and input malicious code or read private data stored on a server.

- **Directory traversal** is an attack that allows access to commands, files and directories that may or may not be connected to the web document root directory. It actually affects the Hypertext Transfer Protocol (HTTP)-based interface.

Zero day exploit

An attack that occurs when the security level of a system is at its lowest, immediately after the discovery of a vulnerability.

Cookie manipulation

An attack where an attacker injects a meta tag in an HTTP header, making it possible to modify a cookie stored in a browser. This is done to impersonate a genuine user or authenticate an attacker to gain access to a website fraudulently.

Locally shared object (LSO) attacks

Also called Flash cookies, LSOs are data that is stored on a user's computer by websites that use Adobe® Flash Player. A site may be able to track a user's browsing behaviour through LSOs causing a breach of privacy.

Attachment attack

An attack where the attacker can merge malicious software or code into a downloadable file or attachment on a web server so that users download and execute it on client systems.

Malicious add-on

An add-on that is meant to look like a normal add-on, except that when a user installs it, malicious content will be injected to target the security loopholes that are present in a web browser.

Header manipulation

An attack where the attacker manipulates the header information passed between the web servers and clients in HTTP requests.

Buffer overflow

An attack in which data goes past the boundary of the destination buffer and begins to corrupt adjacent memory. This causes an app to crash or reboot and may execute rogue code on a system or result in loss of data.

Integer overflow

An attack in which a computed result is too large to fit in its assigned storage space which may lead to crashing or data corruption and may trigger a buffer overflow.

Arbitrary code execution

Also called remote code execution, this is an attack that exploits application vulnerabilities by allowing an attacker to execute any command on a victim's machine and may take complete control over a system.

Network-Based Threats

TCP/IP Basics

Transmission Control Protocol/Internet Protocol (TCP/IP) is a layered suite of many protocols. By adding header information to the data in network packet, a protocol at a given layer on the sending host can communicate with the protocol at the corresponding layer at the receiving host.

TCP/IP Layers

Network Interface / Data Link Layer

Enables the network software to transmit data on the physical network via the network adapter cards and network media.

Internet Layer

Provides addressing, naming and routing.

Internet Protocol (IP): Manages numeric host addresses across the Internet.

Dynamic Host configuration Protocol (DHCP): A separate service that automatically assigns addresses.

Internet Control Message Protocol (ICMP): Tests for communication between devices and sends error messages when the network function is unavailable.

Transport Layer

Provides connection and communication services.

Transport Control Protocol (TCP): A connection-oriented, guaranteed-delivery protocol. It does not only send data, but also waits for acknowledgement (ACK) and fixes errors when possible.

User Datagram Protocol (UDP): Ensures the consistent transmission of data packets (datagrams) by bypassing error checking, which can cause delays and increased processing requirements.

Application Layer

Provides utilities that enable client applications on an individual system to access the networking software.

Network Basic Input Output System (NetBIOS): A simple, broadcast-based naming service.

Sockets: A piece of software within an operating system that connects an application with a network protocol, so that the application can request network services from the operating system.

File Transfer Protocol (FTP): Enables the transfer of files between a user's workstation and a remote host over a TCP network.

IP Port Scanning Attacks

A port scanning attack is a type of network attack where a potential attacker scans the computers and services that are connected to the Internet or other networks to see which TCP and UDP ports are listening and which services on the system are active.

Port Scanning Utilities

There are many utilities available that potential attackers can use to scan ports on networks, including Nmap, SuperScan, strobe and any Telnet client. Many utilities can be downloaded for free from the Internet.

Xmas Attack

The Xmas Scan is available in popular port scanners such as Nmap. It is mainly used to check which machines are active or reachable and subsequently what ports are open or responding so that those machines or ports can be used as an avenue for a follow-up attack.

This type of port scanning uses a Xmas packet with all the flags turned on in the TCP header of the packet. (like Christmas lights)

Eavesdropping Attacks

An eavesdropping attack or sniffing attack uses special monitoring software to gain access to private network communications, either to steal the content of the communication itself or to obtain user names and passwords for future software attacks.

Eavesdropping Utilities

Many utilities are available that will monitor and capture network traffic. Examples of these tools include: Wireshark, the Microsoft Network Monitor Capture utility, tcpdump and dsniff.

Man-in-the-Middle Attacks

A man in the middle attack is a form of eavesdropping where the attacker makes an independent connection between two victims (two clients or a client and a server) and relays information between the two victims as if they are directly talking to each other over a closed connection, when in reality the attacker is controlling the information that travels between the two victims.

Replay Attacks

A replay attack is a network attack where an attacker captures network traffic and stores it for retransmitting at a later time to gain unauthorized access to a specific host or a network. This attack is particularly successful when an attacker captures packets that contain user names, passwords or other authentication data.

Social Network Attacks

Social network attacks are attacks that are aimed at social networking sites such as Facebook, Twitter and LinkedIn.

Evil twin attack and account phishing

An evil twin attack on a social networking site is an attack where an attacker creates a social network account to impersonate a genuine user.

This is often preceded by account phishing, in which an attacker creates an account and joins the friends list of an individual just to try to obtain information about the individual and their circle of friends or colleagues.

Drive-by download

This is a program that is automatically installed on a computer when a user accesses a malicious site, even without clicking a link or giving consent.

Clickjacking

An attack that tricks the user into clicking an unintended link. The attacker uses a combination of visible and invisible HTML frames to fool the user into thinking what they are clicking is what's visible, when in fact the invisible link is layered on top of or beneath the visible frame.

Password stealer

A type of software that, when installed on a system, will be able to capture all the passwords and user names entered into the instant messaging application or social network site that it was designed for.

Spamming

Within social networking, spamming refers to sending unsolicited bulk messages by misusing the electronic messaging services inside the social networking site.

URL Shortening Service

A URL shortening service makes it easier to share links on social networking sites by abbreviating the Uniform Resource Locators

(URLs). The shortened URL hides the true target of the link which attackers exploit.

DoS Attacks

A **Denial of Service (DoS) attack** is a type of network attack in which an attacker attempts to disrupt or disable systems that provide network services by various means.

DoS Targets

The attack can target any service or network device, but s usually mounted against servers or routers, preventing them from responding to legitimate network requests.

DDoS Attacks

A **Distributed Denial of Service (DoS) attack** is a type of DoS attack that uses multiple computers on disparate networks to launch the attack from many simultaneous sources. The attacker introduces unauthorized software that turns the computer into a zombie/drone that directs the computers to launch the attack.

Symptoms of DoS and DDoS Attacks

Overwhelming service requests from hosts outside your network, a sudden and unexplained drop in Internet bandwidth or drain on a specific system resource, causing unusual behavior or freezes.

Types of DoS Attacks

ICMP flood

This attack is based on sending high volumes of ICMP ping packets to a target. Common names are Smurf attacks and ping floods.

UDP flood

In this attack, the attacker attempts to overwhelm the target system with UDP ping requests. Often the source IP address is spoofed, creating a DoS condition for the spoofed IP.

SYN flood

In this attack, an attacker sends countless requests for a TCP connection (SYN messages) to an FTP server, web server or any other target system attached to the Internet.

The target server then responds to each request with a SYN-ACK message and in doing so, creates a space in memory that will be used for the TCP session when the remote host (in this case, the attacker) responds with its own SYN-ACK message.

However, the attacker has crafted the SYN message (usually through IP spoofing) so that the target server sends its initial SYN-ACK response to a computer that will never reply. The targeted server thus reserves memory for numerous TCP connections that will never be completed so eventually floods.

Buffer overflow

A buffer overflow condition is when too much data is fed into a fixed-length memory buffer, resulting in adjacent areas of memory being overwritten. Attackers can cause an exploit with these conditions, introducing bad data into memory, thus opening the door for any number of subsequent attack methods or simply causing the system to cease to function or respond.

A buffer overflow can also occur when there is an excessive amount of incomplete fragmented traffic on a network.

Reflected DoS attack

In reflected DoS and DDoS attacks, a forged source IP address is used when sending requests to a large number of computers. This causes those systems to send a reply to the target system, causing a DoS condition.

Permanent DoS attack

Permanent DoS attacks, also called phlashing, target the actual hardware of a system in order to prevent the victim from easily recovering from a denial of service.

Session Hijacking

A session hijacking attack involves exploiting a computer in session to obtain unauthorized access to an organization's network or services. It involves stealing an active session cookie that is used to authenticate a user to a remote server and using that to control the session thereafter.

P2P Attacks

Peer-to-peer (P2P) attacks are launched by malware propagating through P2P networks. P2P networks typically have a shared command and control architecture, making it harder to detect an attacker. A P2P attack can be used to launch huge DoS attacks.

ARP Poisoning

Address Resolution Protocol (ARP) is the mechanism by which individual hardware MAC addresses are matched to an IP address on a network. ARP poisoning, also known as ARP spoofing, occurs when an attacker with access to the target network redirects an IP address to the MAC address of a computer that is not the intended recipient.

Switches generally deliver packets based on a unique physical address that is individually assigned to every network adapter board by the adapter's manufacturer.

No two network adapters in the world are supposed to have the same physical address. This address is referred to as MAC address because they operate at the Media Access Control (MAC) sub-layer of the Data Link Layer of the OSI network model.

Transitive Access Attacks

Transitive access is the access given to certain members in an organization to use data on a system without the need for authenticating themselves.

The information regarding the list of members that have transitive access is usually saved in a log or host file. If an attacker can access and modify the file, then that will give transitive access to all data and programs to the attacker.

A transitive access attack takes advantage of the transitive access given in order to steal or destroy data.

DNS Vulnerabilities

A DNS translates human-readable domain names into their corresponding IP addresses.

DNS poisoning

In this technique, an attacker exploits the traditionally open nature of the DNS system to redirect a domain name to an IP address of the attacker's choosing.

DNS hijacking

In this technique, an attacker sets up a rogue DNS server. This rogue DNS server responds to legitimate requests with IP addresses for malicious or non-existent websites.

In some cases, Internet Service Providers (ISPs) have implemented DNS hijacking to serve advertisements to users who attempt to navigate to non-existent domain names.

Legitimate Use of DNS Spoofing

Some network hardware has DNS spoofing capabilities built in to allow routers to act as proxy DNS servers in the event that designated primary DNS servers are unavailable.

Wireless Threats and Vulnerabilities

Wireless Security

Wireless security is any method of securing your wireless LAN network to prevent unauthorized network access and network data theft.

Rogue Access Points

A rogue access point is an unauthorized wireless access point on a corporate or private network. They can allow man-in-the-middle attacks and access to private information.

Evil Twins

Evil twins in the context of wireless networking are access points on a network that fool users into believing they are legitimate. Evil twins trick the user to think the wireless signal is genuine, making it difficult to differentiate from a valid access point with the same name.

Jamming

In wireless networking, jamming, also called interference, is an attack in which radio waves disrupt 802.11 wireless signals. Attackers may use a radio transceiver to intercept transmissions and inject jamming packets, disrupting the normal flow of traffic across a network.

Bluejacking

Bluejacking is a method used by attackers to send out unwanted Bluetooth signals from smartphones, mobile phones, tablets and laptops to other Bluetooth-enabled devices.

Bluesnarfing

Bluesnarfing is a method in which attackers gain access to unauthorized information on a wireless device using a Bluetooth connection within the 30-foot Bluetooth transmission limit.

Near Field Communication

Near Field Communication (NFC) is a standard of communication between mobile devices like smartphones and tablets in very close proximity, usually when touching or being only a few inches apart from each other.

War Driving and War Chalking

War driving is the act of searching for instances of wireless networks using wireless tracking devices such as smartphones, tablets, mobile phones or laptops. It locates wireless access points while travelling, which can be exploited to obtain unauthorized Internet access and potentially steal data.

War chalking is the act of using symbols to mark off a sidewalk or wall to indicate that there is an open wireless network that may be offering Internet access.

War Driving Tools

There are common tools that can be used for war driving and war chalking:

- NetStumbler
- Kismet
- Aircrack

IV Attacks

In encryption, an initialization vector (IV) is a number added to a key that constantly changes in order to prevent identical text from producing the same exact ciphertext upon encryption. This makes it more difficult for a hacker to decipher encrypted information that gets repeated.

An IV attack allows the attacker to predict or control the initialization vector in order to bypass this effect. IVs are often compromised if they are constructed with a relatively small bit length. For example, modern systems often have little trouble cracking an IV of 24-bit size.

Packet Sniffing

Packet sniffing can be used as an attack on wireless networks where an attacker captures data and registers data flows, which allow the attacker to analyze the data contained in a packet.

Wireless Replay Attacks

With weak or no wireless encryption, an attacker may find it easier to capture packets over a wireless network and replay them in order to manipulate the data stream. Replay attacks can also be used in conjunction with an IV attack to successfully break weak encryption.

Sinkhole Attacks

Sinkhole attacks take advantage of routing on a wireless network by creating a single node through which all traffic goes. This individual node is able to trick the other nodes into redirecting their traffic. The attacker who controls the sinkhole is potentially able to intercept data packets and slow a network to a crawl.

WEP and WPA Attacks

The Wired Equivalent Privacy (WEP) algorithm came in 64-bit, 128-bit and 256-bit key sizes. Because it used a stream cipher to encrypt data, it relied on an initialization vector (IV) to randomize identical strings of text. With a 24-bit IV size, WEP was extremely vulnerable to an IV attack that would be able to predict the IV value. WEP was deprecated in 2004 and should not be used.

Wi-Fi Protected Access (WPA) protocol generates a 128-bit key for each individual packet sent, which prevents easy cracking of encrypted information. Although WPA used the same stream cipher, WPA2 uses the more secure AES block cipher for encryption.

WPS Attacks

The Wi-Fi Protected Setup (WPS) feature added more methods to authenticate key generation. An 8-digit pin is displayed on the physical wireless device and must be entered in order to enroll in the network. It thus only takes a few thousand guesses to successfully crack the PIN. This can be done in mere hours.

This is a serious flaw in both WPA and WPA2. The feature is on by default on many wireless devices and should be disabled.

Physical Threats and Vulnerabilities

Physical Security

Physical security refers to the implementation and practice of various control mechanisms that are intended to restrict physical access to facilities.

Physical Security Threats and Vulnerabilities

Internal

Disgruntled employees may be a source of physical sabotage of important security-related resources.

External

Risks posed by external power failures should be mitigated by implementing an uninterruptible power supply (UPS) or a generator.

Natural

Buildings and rooms that contain important computing assets should be protected against likely weather-related problems, including tornadoes, hurricanes, snow storms and floods.

Man-made

Whether intentional or accidental. People can cause a number of physical threats.

Hardware Attacks

A hardware attack is an attack that targets a computer's physical components and peripherals, including its hard disk, motherboard, network cabling or smart card reader.

Keylogging Attacks

Keylogging uses software or hardware to capture each keystroke a user types. It may capture passwords as well as other sensitive data. Hardware such as KeyGhost and KeyGrabber are designed to perform keylogging.

One way to mitigate the effects of keylogging is to use a keyboard that encrypts the keystroke signals before they are sent to the system unit.

Environmental Threats and Vulnerabilities

Fire

Fire, whether natural or deliberately set, is a serious environmental security threat because it can destroy hardware and therefore the data contained in it.

Hurricanes and tornadoes

Catastrophic weather event such as hurricanes and tornadoes are major security threats due to the magnitude of damage they can cause to hardware and data.

Flood

A flood is another major security threat that can cause as much damage as fire can.

Extreme temperature

Extreme temperatures, especially heat, can cause some sensitive hardware components to melt and degrade, resulting in data loss.

Extreme humidity

Extreme humidity can cause computer components, data storage media and other devices to rust, deteriorate and degrade resulting in data loss.

Chapter 3 – Managing Data,

Application and Host

Security

Manage Data Security

Layered Security

An approach to securing systems and their data against attack that incorporates many different avenues of defense is called layered security.

Defense in Depth

Defense in depth is a tactic that leverages a layered approach to security, but instead of just focusing on the tools used to protect a system and its data, it is used to plan personal training, policy adoption and other, more comprehensive security strategies.

It comes from a military strategy of delaying an enemy's advance rather than meeting them head on. The layers of defense in depth are shown in the figure below.

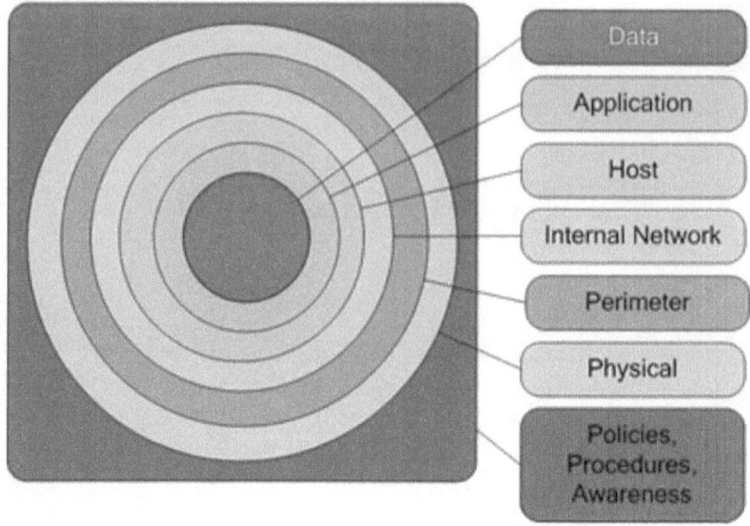

What is Data Security?

Data security refers to the security controls and measures taken to keep an organization's data safe and accessible and to prevent unauthorized access to it. Data Security must be applied at:

- The physical environment
- All devices and systems
- All mobile devices

Data Security Vulnerabilities

Data security vulnerabilities can include the increased use of cloud computing to perform job functions, the lack of restricted physical access to data storage systems and the lack of user awareness.

Data leakage refers to gaining access to data through unintentional user methods such as email and instant messaging and the use of mobile devices.

Data Storage Methods

Common data storage methods include:

- Traditional network servers
- Network-attached storage (NAS)
- Storage area networks (SANs)
- Cloud-based storage

Data Encryption Methods

In order to protect data from security vulnerabilities, you should apply a data encryption method that is appropriate to the data level, including:

- Full disk encryption
- Database encryption
- File encryption
- Removable media encryption
- Mobile device encryption
- Email encryption e.g. Secure/Multipurpose Internet Mail Extensions (S/MIME), Pretty Good Privacy (PGP) and GNU Privacy Guard (GPG)
- Voice encryption

Hardware-Based Encryption Devices

In hardware-based encryption devices, encryption, decryption and access control are enforced by a cryptographic module called a Hardware Security Module (HSM). The devices do not allow execution of external programs that attempt to either reset any counters or access their memory.

Types of Hardware-Based Encryption Devices

Trusted Platform Module (TPM)

This specification includes the use of cryptoprocessors to create a secure computing environment. A TPM can generate cryptographic keys securely and can be used to authenticate hardware, for disk encryption, for digital rights management or for any other encryption-enabled application.

HSM

A cryptoprocessor device that can be attached to servers and computers to provide digital key security.

USB encryption

Users who store sensitive data on USB devices should take care to protect the devices physically.

Hard drive encryption

Hard drive encryption is a full disk encryption method used to encrypt and protect data on the entire disk.

Data States

Security controls need to protect data no matter what state it is in.

At rest

Data at rest refers to data in storage, whether in a database, on a disk or on another storage medium. Data at rest encryption methods include:

PGP Whole Encryption

Microsoft® Windows® BitLocker® disk encryption

OS X® FileVault®

Database encryption for database systems such as MySQL® and Oracle®

TrueCrypt®

In transit

Data in transit refers to data that is moving across a network, including data for web applications, mobile device apps and instant messaging. There are several encryption methods that protect data in transit, also called transport encryption:

- HTTPS/Secure Sockets Layer/Transport Layer Security (SSL/TLS)
- Wi-Fi Protected Access 2 (WPA2)
- Virtual private networks (VPNs)
- Internet Protocol Security (IPSec)
- Secure Shell (SSH)

In use

Data in use refers to any data that is not at rest and not in transit. This includes data being generated, changed, erased or viewed at exactly one network node. You may mitigate the risks by protecting the swap space, hardening the OS and implementing a web proxy.

Permissions and Access Control Lists

You can use file and folder permissions to designate who can read or change data in a file or folder, but on the enterprise level, it can be impossible to manage millions of individual files and folders.

Access Control Lists (ACLs) enable you to restrict access to resources like files and folders and they are commonly implemented as Media Access control (MAC) address filters on wireless routers and access points.

Handling Big Data

Big data refers to data collections that are so large and complex that they are difficult for traditional database tools to manage. Restricting authorized users' visibility will keep them from seeing the data set as a whole and limit them to focusing on only what they need to.

Data Policies

Data protection policies help to clearly define employee responsibilities for protecting personal data that is held by the organization in any form and for any reason. You may encounter policies for:

- Wiping
- Disposing
- Retention
- Storage

Guidelines for Managing Data Security

- Layered security model to address threats and vulnerabilities.

- Identify all data storage forms and security controls to protect them such as encryption, permissions and ACLs.
- For cloud-based storage, ensure the security practices align with organization needs.
- Implement controls to protect data in transit, use and at rest.
- Develop and implement policies to protect data and allow it access simultaneously.

Manage Application Security

What is Application Security?

Application security ensures that the proper development, deployment and maintenance of software is in place to protect applications from threats and vulnerabilities. It is applied in every phase of the software development process and should be incorporated into the initial design of all applications.

Patch Management

Patch management is the practice of monitoring for, obtaining, evaluating, testing and deploying software patches and updates.

Application Security Methods

Configuration baseline

A baseline is composed of the minimum security requirements needed for an application to be complete.

Application hardening

This is the process used to configure a default application to prevent security threats and vulnerabilities.

Patch management

A patch management system is utilized for third party software to ensure that every application is running with the latest security requirements and updates issued by the manufacturers.

Input validation

Input validation involves ensuring that the data entered into a field or variable in an application is within acceptable bounds for the object that will receive the data.

Input Validation Vulnerabilities

Websites and web-based applications are tempting targets for attackers to use input validation attacks on because they are often developed by inexperienced coders or put together in a hurry, with little thought to application or data security.

Command Injection

Command injection is when an attacker sends additional commands to an application through an unchecked input field.

Client-Side and Server-Side Validation

Client-side validation involves performing all input validation and error recovery from within the browser by using JavaScript, Asynchronous JavaScript and XML (AJAX), VBScript or HTML 5 attributes.

Server-side validation involves performing all input validations and error recovery at the server by using a scripting language such as Perl, PHP or ASP.

Error and Exception Handling

Error and exception handling is a strategy organizations use to design and develop security measures that are targeted at possible errors in an application. This type of development strategy is used to prevent attackers from gathering and using sensitive data that may be presented in an error message when the application fails under normal working conditions.

XSS

In a cross-site scripting (XSS) attack, the attacker takes advantage of scripting and input validation vulnerabilities in an interactive website to attack legitimate users in two different ways.

In a stored attack, the attacker injects malicious code or links into a website's forums, databases or other data. When a user views the stored malicious code or clicks a malicious link, an attack is perpetrated against the user.

In a reflected attack, the attacker poses as a legitimate user and sends information to a web server in the form of a page request or form submission. When the web server responds to the request, the attack is directed at the targeted user or users.

XSRF

In a cross-site request forgery (XSRF) attack, an attacker takes advantage of the trust established between an authorized user of a website and the website itself. This type of attack exploits a web browser's trust in a user's unexpired browser cookies.

Cross-Site attack Prevention Methods

- Do not allow HTML formatting in form fields.
- Use input validation on all fields, strings, variables and cookies
- Limit the expiration time for cookies and do not unnecessarily store data in cookies.
- Encrypt data communication between clients and servers.
- Inform end users to not use the Remember Me option when authenticating on websites.

Fuzzing

Fuzzing is a testing method used to identify vulnerabilities and weaknesses in applications by sending the application a range of random or unusual input data and noting any failures and crashes that result.

Fuzzing tools

Pre-built fuzzing tools help generate the fuzzy input data for testing procedures. Some of the best known include SPIKE Proxy and Peach Fuzzer™ Framework.

Web Browser Security

Popular web browsers include Microsoft Edge®, Microsoft Internet Explorer®, Mozilla Firefox®, Apple Safari® and Google Chrome™.

Security features include:

- Pop-up blocker
- Parental controls
- Automated updating
- Encryption

- Proxy support
- Web content
- Advanced security

Guidelines for Establishing Web Browser Security

- Harden the host machine or device
- Install all the latest software versions and patches
- Configure the security settings built in to the software
- Disable scripting when appropriate
- Disable auto-complete and password saving features
- Install anti-malware software

NoSQL Databases

A NoSQL database is a database that provides data storage and retrieval in a non-relational manner. Instead of using tables and relationships between tables, they use a variety of other models:

- Key-value stores store each item in the database as an attribute name or key along with the associated value.
- Document stores contain documents that have standard encoding such as XML and are assigned a key for key-value type lookups.
- Graph stores contain information about networks such as social connections.
- Column stores contain information from very large datasets that store columns of data together, as opposed to the more traditional row-based storage.

Database Security

For relational databases, security measures include:

- Role-based security configuration parameters
- Encrypted communications
- Access control for rows and fields

- User level permissions for stored procedures

Guidelines for Managing Application Security

- Establish security configuration baselines for applications used.
- Identify ways to harden applications.
- Implement a patch management system for applications.
- For applications that require user input, implement input validation controls.
- Implement a combination of client and server side validation for the client-server apps.
- Implement error and exception handling for in-house developed applications.
- Protect against XSS and XSRF attacks.
- Protect relational and NoSQL databases and the applications that rely on their data.

Manage Device and Host Security

To properly protect an organization's assets as a whole, you must be able to secure its networks, devices and end user systems.

Hardening

Hardening is a general term for any security technique in which the default configuration of a system is altered in an attempt to close vulnerabilities and generally protect the system against attacks.

Operating system Security

There can never be a single comprehensive list of vulnerabilities for each operating system, so security professionals must stay up-to-date with system security information posted on vendor websites and in other security references.

Operating system Security Settings

These include:

- Managing services running on the operating system.
- Configuring the operating system's built-in firewall.
- Configuring Internet security options.
- Managing all automatic updates and patches for software and services.
- Enabling necessary auditing and logging functions when applicable.

TCB

The Trusted Computing Base (TCB) is a hardware, firmware and software component of a computer system that is responsible for ensuring that the security policy is implemented and the system is secure. The TCB is implemented in the hardware through processor rings or privileges, in the firmware through driver and resource protection and in the operating system's isolation of resources and services from applications, which is referred to as a Trusted Operating System (TOS).

Security Baselines

A security baseline is a collection of security and configuration settings that are to be applied to a particular host in the enterprise.

Tools are available to scan for and detect a very wide range of vulnerabilities ranging from port scanners to password analyzers to tools that scan for specific hard-to-detect vulnerabilities. Two such tools for Unix are Nessus® and Nmap. When dealing with Microsoft-based systems, tools such as the Microsoft Baseline Security

Analyzer (MBSA) and the Security Configuration Wizard (SCW) are good places to start.

Software Updates

Patch

A small unit of supplemental code meant to address either a security problem or a functionality flaw in a software package or operating system.

Hotfix

A patch that is often issued on an emergency basis to address a specific security flaw.

Rollup

A collection of previously issued patches and hotfixes, usually meant to be applied to one component of a system, such as the web browser or a particular service.

Service Pack

A larger compilation of system updates that can include functionality enhancements, new features and typically all patches, updates and hotfixes issued up to the point of the Service Pack's release.

Application Blacklisting and Whitelisting

Application blacklisting is the practice of preventing the execution of programs that an organization has deemed to be undesirable, whether due to security issues or for any other reason.

Conversely, in application whitelisting, you would maintain a list of approved applications and only those applications would be permitted to be installed or run on the target system. Whitelisting is a good example of the principle of implicit deny.

Logging

Logging is using an operating system or application to record data about activity on a computer. The resulting log files are usually stored as text files in known locations. The level of detail available in log files can vary from showing only significant errors to the recording of every keystroke, mouse movement and network packet.

Auditing

Computer security auditing is the process of performing an organized technical assessment of the security strengths and weaknesses of a system. Computer security audits can include reviewing log files – either manually or via software - testing the strength of passwords, scanning the network for open ports or rogue servers and workstations, reviewing user and group permissions and the physical security related to the system or systems in question.

Anti-malware Software

Anti malware software is protective software that scans individual computers and entire enterprise networks for known viruses, Trojans, worms and other malicious programs.

Types of Anti-malware Software

Antivirus software

An application that scans files for executable code that matches specific patterns known to be common to viruses and monitors systems for activity that is associated with viruses, such as accessing the boot sector.

Anti-spam

Spam prevention may include an anti-spam filtering program that detects and rejects words commonly used in spam messages although issues may arise if a legitimate message is rejected. The IP addresses of known spammers may be blocked to reduce spam mail. Examples of anti-spam software include SPAMfighter, iHateSpam, Cloudmark for Microsoft Outlook® and BullGuard™ Internet Security Suite.

Anti-spyware

This software is specifically designed to protect systems against spyware attacks Examples include Webroot® Spy Sweeper and STOPzilla AntiMalware.

Pop-up blockers

Pop-ups are windows or frames that load and appear automatically when a user connects to a particular web page. *Pop-up blockers* prevent pop-ups from sites that are unknown or untrusted and prevent the transfer of unwanted code to the local system.

Host-based firewalls

This is software that is installed on a single system to specifically guard against networking attacks.

Windows Firewall configuration

Windows Firewall is a software-based firewall that is included with all current Windows operating system client and server versions. You may configure the firewall using the program in the *Control Panel* or through *Group Policy* settings.

Types of Firewall Rules

Inbound rules

These rules define the action to be performed by the firewall on the data that enters the system from another system.

Outbound rules

These rules define the action to be performed by the firewall on the data that flows out of the systems.

Communication security rules

These rules define the type of authentication that is needed to allow communication between the systems.

Virtualization Security Techniques

Patch management

A patch management system must be in place to ensure that all relevant patches are installed.

Least privilege

The concept of least privilege should be applied when determining access control assignments to any virtual environment

Logging

User activities in the virtual environment should be logged and reviewed to check for irregular activity and any possible security breaches.

Design

Applying good security measures to all virtualization environments starts with a good design.

Snapshots

Consistently capturing snapshots or the state a virtual environment is in at a certain point in time, will provide you with a quick and easy way to recover the entire environment should it be compromised or degrade in performance.

Host availability

Also called host elasticity, the availability of a virtual host is dependent on its ability to adapt to various system changes.

Sandboxing

Sandboxing is the practice of isolating an environment from a larger system in order to guarantee that the environment runs in a controlled, secure fashion.

Hardware Security Controls

- Proper logoff and shutdown procedures.
- Wireless communication approval by IT department.
- Mobile devices secured safely when not used.
- Cable locks on all end user hardware components.
- Strong password policies.

Non-standard Hosts

Supervisory control and data acquisition (SCADA) systems

A type of industrial control system that monitors and controls industrial processes such as manufacturing and fabrication; infrastructure processes such as power transmission and distribution; and facility processes such as energy consumption and HVAC systems.

Embedded-software systems

Hosts such as game consoles, printers, Smart TVs and motor vehicles include software not meant to be updated or not normally by IT.

Highly stable and reliable computers that are used for mission critical applications and bulk data processing.

Mobile devices such as smartphones and tablets may be considered non-standard hosts if their Android or iOS versions are old enough to no longer be supported by the manufacturer.

Security Controls for non-standard Hosts

Are considered to be static environments, which are operating systems and other computing environments that are not updated or changed, either by design or due to other circumstances such as age.

- Layered security, including network segmentation and application firewalls.
- Manual updates on an ad hoc basis for old mobile OS.
- Firmware version control for SCADA and embedded systems.
- Wrappers, which are software that contains other data or software, such as legacy code to enable the contained data to operate in newer environments.
- Controlling redundancy (the provision of multiple identical instances of a system for fault tolerance) and diversity (the provision of multiple different implementations of the same specification to minimize common vulnerabilities).

Strong Passwords

A strong password is a password that meets the complexity requirements that are set by a system administrator and documented in a security policy or password policy.

Password complexity requirements should specify:

- The minimum length of password.
- Required characters, such as a combination of letters, numbers and symbols.
- Forbidden character strings, such as the user account name or dictionary words.

Guidelines for Establishing Device and Host Security

Device Security Guidelines

- Harden the operating system to close security holes, for software based systems.
- Install the latest firmware updates for hardware based systems.
- Implement hardware and software manufacturers' security recommendations.
- Implement strict access controls and use strong, robust passwords.
- Secure router configuration files.
- Configure ingress and egress filters to help prevent IP spoofing and DoS attacks.
- Disable IP source routing to prevent attackers specifying the path the packets take through the network.
- Implement a routing protocol that supports authentication, such as Routing Information Protocol (RIP) version 2 (RIPv2), Enhanced Interior Gateway Routing Protocol

(EIGRP) or Open Shortest Path First (OSPF) to prevent unauthorized changes to routing tables.

- Protect routers, virtual local area networks (VLANs), Network Address Translation (NAT) devices and other internetworking devices with properly configured firewalls.
- Protect against Address Resolution Protocol (ARP) poisoning by verifying that all routers are configured properly and set up with notifications and appropriate monitoring software.
- Implement NAT to hide the true IP scheme of your network.
- Close unused well-known Transmission Control Protocol (TCP) and User Datagram Protocol (UDP) ports.
- Place appropriate servers in a demilitarized zone (DMZ).
- Disable IP directed broadcasts on routers.
- Protect all internetwork devices and network media from unauthorized physical access.
- Test functionality of systems after hardening to make sure required services and resources are available.
- Document your changes.

Host Security Guidelines

- Require strong passwords to protect against password-cracking utilities.
- Implement manufacturers' security recommendations.
- Implement antivirus, anti-spyware and anti-adware software.
- Disable unnecessary services to prevent attackers from exploiting them.
- Restrict access permissions to users who absolutely need access.
- Implement security policies to control, limit or restrict user interaction.

- Physically secure mission-critical servers and devices in locked rooms with access to only trusted administrators.
- Plan backup strategies and methods to restore data in the vent of data loss or corruption. Store backup media offsite for business continuity.
- Test system functions after hardened.
- Utilize scanning and auditing tools to detect vulnerabilities.
- Identify non-standard hosts and measures to protect them.
- Document changes.

Manage Mobile Security

Mobile Device Types

A mobile device is a small handheld computing device.

Mobile Device Vulnerabilities

Mobile devices have the ability to transfer data and access the Internet. With such functions threats exist e.g. viruses and spam. If a mobile device is lost or stolen, attackers could hack in the device and access sensitive information.

Mobile Device Security Controls

- Use device management
- Enable screen lock
- Require a strong password
- Configure device encryption
- Require remote wipe/sanitization/lockout
- Enable global positioning system (GPS) tracking
- Enforce application control
- Use asset tracking and inventory control
- Limit removable storage capabilities
- Implement storage segmentation

- Disable unused features

Mobile Application Security Controls

- Encryption and key management
- Credential management
- Authentication and transitive trust
- Restrict geo-tagging
- Application whitelisting

BYOD Controls

- Corporate policies and acceptable use policies
- On-boarding and off-boarding employees
- Decide on data ownership and support ownership
- Patch management and antivirus management
- Consider architecture and infrastructure needs
- Forensics
- Privacy
- Control for on-board camera, microphone and video use

Guidelines for Managing Mobile Security

- Be familiar of different mobile devices and operating systems.
- Implement a centralized managing system.
- Enforce screen lock, password input and other device access features.
- Disable unnecessary features.
- Plan for remote wipe or lock out data in case of theft.
- Enable device-wide encryption.
- Apply access and application control on all devices.

- Manage how data is stored and restrict storage.
- Make a device inventory.
- Consider employees' BYOD needs.
- Draft rules and regulations for mobile use.
- Acclimate new employees to the protocols and plan for off-boarding former employees.
- Consider BYOD legal issues: data ownership, privacy concerns, quantity of device usage controllable.
- Adjust system architecture and infrastructure as required.
- When developing apps, enforce proper encryption and key management protocols.
- Select proper authentication methods and credential management systems.
- Restrict what apps communicate with and how.

Chapter 4- Implementing

Network Security

Configure Security Parameters on Network Devices and Technologies

Network Components

Device

Any piece of hardware such as a computer, server, printer or smartphone.

Media

Connects devices to the network and carries data between devices.

Network adapter

Hardware that translates the data between the network and a device.

Network operating system

Software that controls network traffic and access to network resources.

Protocol

Software that controls network communications using a set of rules.

Network Devices

Router

A device that connects multiple networks that use the same protocol and determines the most efficient path for data to take. Most routers will not forward broadcast network traffic.

Switch

A device that has multiple network ports and combines multiple physical network segments into a single logical network. Standard switches generally forward broadcasts to all ports on the switch, but will send individual packets to the specific destination host based on the unique physical address assigned to each network adapter. Some switches can perform routing functions based on protocol addresses.

Proxy Server

A system that can isolate networks from the Internet by downloading and storing Internet files on behalf of internal clients. A proxy server can include Network Address Translation (NAT) and firewall functionality.

Firewall

Any software or hardware device that protects a system or network by blocking unwanted network traffic. There are three common types of firewalls:

Host or personal firewalls are installed on a single computer and are used to secure most home computers.

Network-based firewalls are dedicated hardware/software combinations that protect all the computers on a network behind the firewall.

Web application-based firewalls are specifically deployed to secure an organization's web-based applications and transactions from attackers.

Load balancer

A network device that performs load balancing as its primary function. Load balancing is the practice of spreading out the work among the devices in a network.

All-in-one security appliance

A single network security device that is used to perform a number of security functions to secure a network.

Multifunction Network Devices

A multifunction network device is any piece of network hardware that is meant to perform more than one networking task without having to be reconfigured.

Application Aware Devices

An application aware device is a network device that manages the information of any applications that interface with it.

Router Discovery Protocols

Routing Information Protocol (RIP)

A simple distance –vector protocol that is easy to configure. It is best deployed in small networks with only a few routers in an environment that does not change as much.

RIPv2

Enhances RIP by supporting the following features:

Next Hop Addressing: Includes Internet Protocol (IP) address information in routing tables for every router in a given path to avoid sending packets through extra routers.

Authentication: Enables password authentication and the use of a key to authenticate routing information to a router.

Subnet mask: Supports more subnets and hosts on an internetwork by supporting Variable Length Subnet Masks (VLSMs) and including length information in routing information.

Multicast packet: Decreases the workload of non-RIPv2 hosts by communicating only with RIPv2 routers. RIPv2 packets use 224.0.0.9 as their multicast address.

Interior Gateway Routing Protocol (IGRP)

This is a distance-vector routing protocol developed by Cisco as an improvement over RIP and RIPv2. It was designated as a protocol best deployed on interior routers within an autonomous system (AS).

Enhanced Interior Gateway Routing Protocol (EIGRP)

This is a proprietary routing protocol developed by Cisco and is considered a hybrid protocol. It includes features that support VLSM and classful and classless subnet masks.

Network Analysis Tools

Sniffer

A device or program that monitors network communications on the network wire or across a wireless network and captures data. A sniffer can be used to gather information passed through a network or to selectively record specific types of transactions based on devices, protocols or applications used.

Spam filters

Programs used to read and reject incoming messages that contain target words and phrases used in known spam messages.

Protocol analyzer

Also known as a network analyzer, this is a type of diagnostic software that can examine and display data packets that are being transmitted over a network. Protocol analyzers can gather all the information passed through a network or selectively record certain types of transactions based on various filtering mechanisms.

IDS

An intrusion detection system (IDS) is a detection control system that scans, audits and monitors the security infrastructure for signs of attacks in progress. IDS software can also analyze data and alert security administrators to potential infrastructure problems.

NIDS

A network intrusion detection system (NIDS) is a type of IDS that primarily uses passive hardware sensors to monitor traffic on a specific segment of the network. It cannot analyze encrypted packets because it has no method for decrypting the data. It can sniff traffic and send alerts about anomalies and concerns. One particular use of NIDS is rogue machine detection. A *rogue machine* is any unknown or unrecognized device that is connected to a network, often with malicious intent.

WIDS

A *wireless IDS (WIDS)* is a type of NIDS that scans the radio frequency spectrum for possible threats to the wireless network, primarily rogue access points. A WIDS usually compares the Media Access Control (MAC) address of a device that acts as an access point to known addresses, and if it doesn't find a match, it gives out an alert. However, MAC address spoofing can complicate the efficacy of WIDS.

IPS

An intrusion prevention system (IPS) has the monitoring capability of an ids, but actively works to block any detected threats. This allows an IPS to take the extra steps necessary to prevent an intrusion into a system.

NIPS

A network intrusion prevention system (NIPS) monitors suspicious network and system traffic and reacts in real time to block it. Blocking may involve dropping unwanted data packets or resetting the connection. One advantage of using the NIPS is that it can regulate traffic according to specific content, because it examines packets as they travel through the IPS. This is in contrast to the way a firewall behaves, which blocks IP addresses or entire ports.

WIPS

A wireless IPS (WIPS) is a type of NIPS that scans the radio frequency spectrum for possible threats to the wireless network, primarily rogue access points and can actively block this malicious traffic. Like a NIPS, a WIPS can drop undesired packets in real time as they come in through the network.

Types of Network Monitoring Systems

Behavior based monitoring

This system detects changes in normal operating data sequences and identifies abnormal sequences. When first installed, they have no performance baseline or acceptable traffic threat. However, over time they learn which traffic is allowed and which isn't with the administrator's assistance.

Signature-based monitoring

This solution uses a predefined set of rules provided by a software vendor to identify traffic that is unacceptable.

Anomaly-based monitoring

This system uses a database of unacceptable traffic patterns identified by analyzing traffic flows. Anomaly-based systems are dynamic and create a performance baseline of acceptable traffic flows during their implementation process.

Heuristic monitoring

This system is set up using known best practices and characteristics in order to identify and fix issues within the network.

VPNs

A virtual private network (VPN) is a private network that is configured by tunneling through a public network, such as the Internet. VPNs provide secure connections between endpoints, such as routers, clients or servers by using tunneling to encapsulate and encrypt data. Special VPN protocols are required to provide the VPN tunneling, security and data encryption services.

VPN Concentrator

A VPN concentrator is a single device that incorporates advanced encryption and authentication methods in order to handle a large number of VPN tunnels. It is geared specifically toward secure remote access or sit-to-site VPNs. VPN concentrators provide high performance, high availability and impressive scalability.

Web Security Gateways

A web security gateway is a utility used primarily to intentionally block internal Internet access to a predefined list of websites or categories of websites. The utility is configured by administrators to deny access to a specified list of Uniform Resource Locators (URLs) by URL filtering.

Blacklists

Blacklists contain addresses that are automatically blocked. URL filtering functions use the entries in a blacklist to allow or deny access to a particular website. When a URL is specified on a whitelist, access is allowed and when a URL is specified on a greylist, temporary access is granted.

Network Design Elements and Components

NAC

Network Access Control (NAC) is a general term for the collected protocols, policies and hardware that govern access on device network interconnections. NAC provides an additional security layer that scans systems for conformance and allows or quarantines updates to meet policy standards.

Note: *Network Access Protection (NAP)* is the Microsoft implementation of NAC.

DMZs

A demilitarized zone (DMZ) is a small section of a private network that is located between two firewalls and made available for public access. A DMZ enables external clients to access data on private systems such as web servers, without compromising the security of the internal network as a whole. The external or perimeter firewall enables public clients to access the service; the internal firewall prevents them from connecting to protected internal hosts.

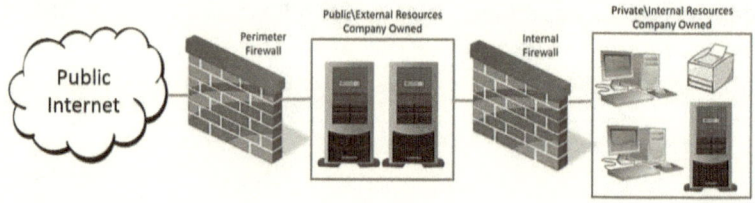

VLANs

A virtual local area network (VLAN) is a point-to-point logical network that is created by grouping selected hosts together, regardless of their physical location. A VLAN uses a switch or router that controls the groups of hosts that receive network broadcasts. VLANs provide network security by enabling administrators to segment groups of hosts within the larger physical network.

VLAN Vulnerabilities

Improperly configured VLAN devices and associated switches give attackers the opportunity to redirect packets from one VLAN to another (through VLAN hopping) and to capture those packets and the data they contain. Some VLAN switch configurations can also be open to other attacks such as Denial of Service (DoS), traffic flooding and MAC address spoofing.

Subnetting

Subnetting is a network design element that is used to divide a large network into smaller logical networks. Each node is configured with an IP address and a subnet address in order to segment a network into subnetworks and to create a routing structure.

NAT

Network Address Translation (NAT) is a simple form of Internet security that conceals internal addressing schemes from the public Internet. A router is configured with a single public IP address on its external interface and a private, non-routable address on its internal interface. A NAT service translates between the two addressing schemes. Packets sent to the Internet from internal hosts all appear as if they came from a single IP address, preventing external hosts from identifying and connecting directly to internal systems.

Remote Access

Remote access is the ability to connect to network systems and services from an offsite or remote location. Remote access is often most secure when users are able to connect through a VPN.

Telephony

Telephony provides voice communications through devices over a distance. Common telephony components include:

- Voice over Internet Protocol (VoIP) implementation, in which voice traffic is transmitted over the IP network.
- Private branch exchange implementations.

- *Computer telephony integration (CTI),* which incorporates telephone, email, web and computing infrastructures.

Virtualization

Virtualization technology separates computing software from the hardware it runs on via an additional software layer. It provides flexibility and hardware utilization by running multiple operating systems on a single computer, each thinking it is the only system present. Virtualization allows hardware resources to be pooled and leveraged as part of a virtual infrastructure, increasing available processing and storage capacity.

Cloud Computing

Cloud computing is a method of computing that involves real-time communication over large networks to provide the resources, software, data and media needs of a user, business or organization.

Cloud Computing Deployment Methods

Private

Private cloud services are usually distributed by a single company or other business entity over a private network.

Public

Public cloud computing is done over the Internet by organizations that offer their services to general consumers.

Community

When multiple organizations share ownership of a cloud service, they are deployed as a community cloud.

Hybrid

Hybrid cloud computing combines two or more of the deployment methods into one entity.

Cloud Computing Service Types

Software

Software as a Service (SaaS) refers to using the cloud to provide applications to users. Examples include Microsoft Office ® 365™. Salesforce® and Genial™.

Platform

Platform as a Service (PaaS) refers to using the cloud to provide virtual systems such as operating systems to customers. Examples include Oracle® Database, Microsoft Windows Azure™ SQL Database and Google App Engine™.

Infrastructure

Infrastructure as a Service (IaaS) refers to using the cloud to provide access to any or all infrastructure needs a client may have. Examples include Amazon® Elastic Compute Cloud®, Microsoft Windows Azure Virtual Machines and OpenStack™

Implement Networking Protocols and Services

The OSI Model

The Open Systems Interconnection (OSI) model is a way to abstract how a network is structured based on how it communicates with other elements in the network. These elements are divided into seven discrete layers with a specific order.

Physical

Defines connections between devices and physical transmission media.

Data link

Provides a link between two directly connected nodes, as well as detecting and fixing errors in the physical layer. Point-to-Point Protocol (PPP) is a connection protocol that provides encryption, authentication and compression between nodes. G.hn is a standard that defines telephony networking over power lines and coaxial cables.

Network

Provides the protocols for transferring data from one node to another in a system with multiple nodes with unique addresses. Internet Protocol (IP) manages numeric host addresses across the Internet. Internet Control Message Protocol (ICMP) tests for communication between devices and sends error messages when network function is unavailable. Routing Information Protocol (RIP) prevents loops in routing by limiting the number of intermediary devices between a source and its destination.

Transport

Controls the reliability of data transmission between nodes on a network for the benefit of the higher layers. Transmission Control Protocol (TCP) is a connection-oriented, guaranteed-delivery protocol which means that it not only sends data, but also waits for acknowledgements (ACK) and fixes errors when possible. User Datagram Protocol (UDP) ensures the consistent transmission of data packets (datagrams) by bypassing error checking which can cause delays and increased processing requirements. Stream Control Transmission Protocol (SCTP) combines the features of TCP and UDP into one protocol.

Session

Controls the connections between computers through checkpointing so that connections, when terminated, may be recovered. Network File System (NFS) allows clients to access files on a network as if they were accessing local storage. Socket Secure (SOCKS) routes data packets on a network through a proxy server and includes authentication.

Presentation

Transforms data into a format that can be understood by the programs in the application layer above it. Independent Computing Architecture (ICA) specifies the transmission of data between the client and application server.

Application

Allows client interaction with software by identifying resource and communication requirements. Hypertext Transfer Protocol (HTTP) allows the exchange of information across the World Wide Web. File Transfer Protocol (FTP) enables the transfer of files between a user's workstation and a remote host over a TCP network. Domain

Name system (DNS) translates human-intelligible domain names into their corresponding IP addresses.

OSI Model and Security

As a security professional, understanding the layers of the OSI model makes it easier for you to identify threats and their targets, as well as how these threats will impact your network. If the most fundamental layer (physical) fails, then the rest are likely to fail as well. Likewise, if an attack hits a poorly secured application layer, then the

TCP/IP

Transmission Control Protocol / Internet Protocol

This is a non-proprietary, routable network protocol suite that enables computers to communicate over all types of networks. TCP/IP is the native protocol of the Internet and is required for Internet connectivity.

IP version 4 (IPv4)

This is an Internet standard that uses a 32-bit number assigned to a computer on a TCP/IP network. Some of the bits in the address represent the network segment; the other bits represent the computer, or node, itself. Each decimal number can range from 0 to 255, but first number cannot be 0. In addition, all four numbers in a host address cannot be 0 (0.0.0.0) or 255 (255.255.255.255).

IP version 6 (IPv6)

This is an Internet standard that increases the available pool of IP addresses by implementing a 128-bit binary address space. IPv6 also includes new efficiency features, such as simplified address headers, hierarchical addressing, support for time-sensitive network traffic and a new structure for unicast addressing.

IPv6 addresses are usually separated by colons into eight groups of four hexadecimal digits. While all eight groups must have four digits, leading zeros can be omitted and groups of consecutive zeros can be replaced with two colons.

2001:0db8:85a3:0000:0000:8a2e:0370:7334

2001:db8:85a3:0:0:8a2e:370:7334

2001:db8:85a3::8a2e:370:7334

Full adoption of IPv6 will require a conversion of IP routers to support interoperability. It uses an Institute of Electrical and Electronics Engineers (IEEE) standard called Extended Unique Identifier (EUI). A host computer implemented with EUI-64 can assign itself a 64-bit IPv6 interface identifier automatically.

Dynamic Host Configuration Protocol (DHCP)

This is a protocol used to automatically assign IP addressing information to IP network computers. Unless the system has manually assigned static IP addresses, most IP systems obtain addressing information dynamically from a central DHCP server or a router configured to provide DHCP functions.

The IEEE

The Institute of Electrical and Electronics Engineers (IEEE) is an organization dedicated to advancing theory and technology in the electrical sciences, electronic communications, circuitry, computer engineering, electromagnetics and nuclear science.

APIPA (Automatic Private IP Addressing)

Automatic Private IP Addressing (APIPA) is a Microsoft Windows®
service that enables DHCP client computers to initialize TCP/IP when
DHCP is unavailable. APIPA self-allocates addresses randomly from a
small range of 169.254.0.1 to 169.254.255.254.

Simple TCP/IP Services

Simple TCP/IP services is a Microsoft implementation that supports
several TCP/IP services such as Character Generator, Daytime,
Discard and Quote of the Day.

DNS

The Domain Name system (DNS) is the primary name resolution
service on the Internet and private IP networks. DNS is a hierarchical
system of databases that map computer names to their associated
IP addresses.

DNS Security Measures

- Place the DNS Server in the DMZ within the firewall
  perimeter.
- Set firewall rules to block incoming non-essential services
  requests.
- Expose only essential ports.
- Strengthen DHCP filtering.
- Prevent buffer overflows.
- Use Secure Sockets Layer (SSL).
- Keep the DNs updated regularly by OS vendor security
  patches.
- Back up the DNS and save them in different geographical
  locations.

HTTP

Hypertext Transfer Protocol (HTTP) is the TCP/IP protocol that enables clients to connect to and interact with websites. It is responsible for transferring the data on web pages between systems. HTTP defines how messages are formatted and transmitted, as well as what actions web servers and the client's browser should take in response to different commands.

Web Server Security

- Remove unnecessary services running in the background.
- Avoid remote access to web servers.
- Store web applications, website logs that contain user information and other related files on another, secured, drive.
- Install security patches regularly.
- Delete or disable unused user accounts.
- Use the appropriate security tools.
- Use port scanners to scan the web servers regularly.

SSL/TLS

Secure Sockets Layer (SSL) and Transport Layer Security (TLS) are security protocols that combine certificates for authentication with public key data encryption.

TLS vs. SSL

Although often used in conjunction, SSL is a predecessor of TLS. The latest versions of TLS are more secure than SSL, but very few websites currently implement them.

HTTPS

Hypertext Transfer Protocol Secure (HTTPS) is a secure version of HTTP that supports web commerce by providing a secure connection between a web browser and a server. HTTPS uses SSL/TLs to encrypt data and the web address begins with the protocol identifier https://.

SSH

Secure Shell (SSH) is a protocol used for secure remote login and secure transfer of data. To ensure security, the entire SSH session, including authentication, is encrypted using a variety of encryption methods. SSH is the preferred protocol for working with File Transfer Protocol (FTP) and is used primarily on Linux and Unix systems to access shell accounts.

SNMP

Simple Network Management Protocol (SNMP) is a service used to collect information from network devices for diagnostic and maintenance purposes. SNMP includes two components: management systems and agent software, which is installed on network devices such as servers, routers and printers. The agents send information to an SNMP manager. The SNMP manager can then notify an administrator of problems, run a corrective program or script, store the information for later review or ask the agent about a specific network device.

ICMP

Internet Control Message Protocol (ICMP) is an IP network service that reports on connections between two hosts. It is often used for simple functions, such as the ping command that checks for a response from a particular target host. Attackers can use redirected ICMP packets in two ways: to flood a router and cause a DoS attack by consuming resources (Smurf attack) and to reconfigure routing tables by using forged packets.

IPSec

Internet Protocol Security (IPSec) is a set of open, non-proprietary standards that you can use to secure data as it travels across the network or the Internet. IPSec operates at the Internet layer of the TCP/IP model, so the protocol is not application dependent.

IPSec System Support

Many operating systems support IPSec, including Microsoft Windows, Linux, Unix, Sun Solaris etc. Internetworking devices also support it.

IPSec Policies

An IPSec policy is a set of security configuration settings that define how an IPSec-enabled system will respond to IP network traffic. The policy determines the security level and other characteristics for an IPSec connection. Each computer that uses IPSec must have an assigned policy.

Policies work in pairs; each of the endpoints in a network communication must have an IPSec policy with at least one matching security method in order for the communication to succeed.

Some default IPSec policies include secure server, server, client, IP filters, filter action, authentication method, tunnel setting and connection type.

iSCSI

The Internet Small Computer System Interface (iSCSI) is a protocol implementing links between data storage networks using IP. An iSCSI does not inherently provide encryption during transmission, an attacker can monitor these transmissions, alter data or corrupt it.

Fibre Channel

Fibre channel is a protocol designed to link data storage across a network and provide remote access over large distances. It requires installing special-purpose cabling in place of existing infrastructure which makes it expensive but produces greater performance and reliability.

FCoE

Fibre Channel over Ethernet (FCoE) allows traditional Fibre Channel protocols to use high-speed Ethernet networks to transmit and store data. This protocol decreases the infrastructure cost of cabling, as well as lowering the amount of physical hardware devices like network interface cards and switches that are required. Likewise, power and cooling costs may be reduced.

Telnet

Telnet is a network protocol that allows a client to initiate remote command access to a host over TCP/IP. The client runs a Telnet program that can establish a connection with the remote server. Granting the client a virtual terminal into the server.

The Telnet protocol is not encrypted, so packets can be easily analyzed and attackers can eavesdrop on credentialed input. Man-in-the-middle attacks are also relatively easy, as Telnet does not require any sort of authentication between client and host.

NetBIOS

Network Basic Input Output System (NetBIOS) is an interface that allows applications to properly communicate over different computers in a network.

It has 3 basic functions:

- Communication over sessions
- Connectionless communication using datagrams
- Name registration

Attackers can exploit NetBIOS by obtaining information about a system, including registered name IP addresses and operating system/applications used.

To harden NetBIOS against an attack, you should:

- Implement strong password policies
- Limit root access on a network share
- Disable null session capability

File Transfer Protocols

File Transfer Protocol (FTP)

This protocol enables the transfer of files between a user's workstation and a remote host. With FTP, a user can access the directory structure on a remote host, change directories, search and rename files and directories and download and upload files.

Simple File Transfer Protocol (SFTP)

This protocol was an early unsecured file transfer protocol that has since been declared obsolete.

Trivial File Transfer Protocol (TFTP)

This is a very limited protocol used primarily as an automated process of configuring boot files between machines. Because it offers almost no security, this protocol is used primarily on local networks instead of on the Internet.

FTP over SSH

Also called Secure FTP, is a secure version of FTP that uses an SSH tunnel as an encryption method to transfer, access and manage files. It is primarily used on Windows.

Secure Copy Protocol (SCP)

This protocol uses SSH to securely transfer computer files between a local and a remote host or between two remote hosts. SCP can also be implemented as a command-line utility that uses either SCP or SFTP to perform secure copying. It is primarily used on Unix.

File Transfer Protocol Secure (FTPS)

This protocol, also known as FTP-SSL, combines the use of FTP with additional support for SSL/TLs.

Ports and Port Ranges

In networks, a port is the endpoint of a logical connection. All ports are assigned a number in a range from 0 to 65,535. The Internet Assigned Numbers Authority (IANA) separates port numbers into three blocks.

1. Well-known ports (0 - 1,023)

Specific port numbers are most vulnerable to attack.

2. Registered ports (1,024 - 49,151)

Too system-specific for direct target by attackers but they might scan for open ports in this range.

3. Dynamic or private ports (49,125 - 65,535)

Common Default Network Ports

Port	Service
21	FTP (File Transfer Protocol)
22	SSH (Secure Shell)
25	SMTP (Simple mail Transfer Protocol)
53	DNS (Domain Name System)
80	HTTP (Hypertext Transfer Protocol)
110	POP3 (Post Office Protocol)
139	NetBIOS Session Service
143	MAP (Internet Message Access Protocol)
443	HTTPS (Hypertext Transfer Protocol Secure)
3389	RDP (Remote Desktop Protocol)

Apply Secure Network Administration Principles

With proper security administration principles applied, a business can ensure that systems and applications are available to the users who rely on them.

Rule-Based Management

Rule-based management is the use of operational rules or restrictions to govern the security of an organization's infrastructure. Typically, rules are incorporated into organizational policies that get disseminated throughout an organization.

Network Administration Security Methods

Flood Guard

This is a tool used by network administrators and security professionals to protect resources from flooding attacks, such as Distributed Denial of Service (DDoS) attacks. Flood guards should be installed to detect when an attack occurs and apply appropriate mitigation techniques.

Loop protection

Network loops can occur when one or more pathways exist between the endpoints in a network and packets get forwarded over and over again. Proper router configuration must be applied and manufacturer configurations should be verified.

Port Security

Properly securing ports on a network includes:

- Disabling unnecessary services.

- Closing ports that are by default open or have limited functionality.
- Regularly applying the appropriate patches.
- Hiding responses from ports that indicate their status and allow access to pre-configured connections only.

Secure router configuration

Protects your network from attacks and can also prevent routing loops caused by routing algorithm errors.

MAC limiting

MAC limiting is the technique of defining how many different MAC addresses may connect to a network device like a router. When the preset limit is exceeded, the device may trigger a warning, disable new MAC learning or shut down completely, depending on how it is configured.

MAC filtering

MAC filtering is the technique of allowing or denying devices with certain MAC addresses to connect to a network. This may be in the form of a whitelist in which only the MAC addresses specified are granted access or a blacklist in which certain MAC addresses are explicitly blocked.

Network separation

Splitting your network into two or more logically separated networks helps separate critical network functions from lower-priority functions so that security can be managed on a critical versus non-critical basis. It also prevents intruders from getting to other systems and helps enforce access control efforts.

VLAN management

Most organizations will keep track of VLAN configurations using diagrams and documentation.

Implicit deny

Use the principle of implicit deny so that firewall blocks any traffic it does not recognize.

Log analysis

Regular monitoring and analysis of security logs helps detect any unauthorized intrusion attempts on the network. It is also wise to regularly review logs and assess any data leaks and insider threats that may be present.

Unified Threat Management (UTM)

Unified threat management (UTM) refers to a system that centralizes various security techniques - firewall, anti-malware, network intrusion prevention, URL filtering, content inspection, malware inspection etc. – into a single appliance.

When defense is unified under a single system, this creates the potential for a single point of failure that could affect an entire network. UTM system can also struggle with latency issues if they are subject to too much network activity.

Guidelines for Applying Network Security Administration Principles

To apply network security administration principles, you should:

- Manage network devices such as firewalls, routers, switches, load balancers, proxies and other all-in-one appliances to ensure that configurations conform to the security policies.
- Maintain documentation about current server configurations.
- Establish and document baselines that suit your organization.
- Set up strong Access control Lists (ACLs) in sensitive resources on your network and use the principle of implicit deny to ensure that unauthorized users and groups cannot inadvertently access information when they do not have specific rights to do so.
- Update antivirus software regularly. If possible, the task should be automated.
- Configure the required network services only
- Disable unused interfaces and application service ports.
- Have a good backup strategy and disaster recovery plan (DRP) in place.
- Apply security updates and patches regularly.
- Ensure that sensitive data is well encrypted.
- Regularly check event logs for unusual activities.
- Monitor network activities on a regular basis.

Secure Wireless Traffic

Wireless Networks

Wireless networks are, fundamentally, networks that do not rely solely on physical cabling in a network infrastructure. Data is transmitted through low-frequency radio waves in the invisible electromagnetic spectrum.

Wireless Antenna Types

The two main categories of antennas are directional and omni-directional.

Directional antennas transmit signals to a specific point. As a result, they have a large gain or the reliable connection range and power of a signal measured in decibels and they are less susceptible to interference.

Omni-directional antennas send and receive radio waves from all directions, usually as the main distribution source of a wireless signal. These antennas are common on wireless routers and mobile wireless adapters, as these devices require providing or receiving service in all possible directions. The coverage provided by omni-directional antennas limits their gain.

Omni-directional antennas

Rubber duck

A rubber duck or rubber ducky is a small omnidirectional antenna that is usually sealed in a rubber jacket. They have little gain, however, because of their small size, are ideal for mobility. They are used in walkie-talkies, two-way radios, as well as short range wireless networking.

Ceiling dome

The antenna is installed in ceilings and is commonly used to cover rooms in a building with a wireless signal.

Directional antennas

Yagi

Used primarily in radios, but also employed in long distance wireless networking to extend the range of hotspots.

Parabolic

Very precise, used often in satellite dishes, that has a significant amount of gain. Because they are so precise, it is somewhat more difficult to establish a connection with a parabolic antenna.

Backfire

A small antenna that looks similar to a parabolic dish but with less gain. They are used in wireless networks to efficiently target a specific physical area without overextending coverage.

Cantenna

A homemade antenna that can extend wireless networks or help to discover them. They typically involve placing a metal can over another antenna, such as a satellite dish, in an attempt to increase its gain.

802.11 Standards

802.11

A family of specifications developed by the IEEE for wireless LAN communications between wireless devices or between wireless devices and a base station. It specifies wireless data transfer rates of up to 2 megabits per second (Mbps) in the 2.4 gigahertz (GHz) frequency band. The standard is supported by various working groups, known collectively as 802.11x.

802.11a

The specification supports speeds up to 54 Mbps in the 5 GHz frequency band. Unfortunately, the speed has a limited range of only 60 feet.

802.11b

The first specification to be called Wi-Fi and the least expensive wireless network protocol. It provides for an 11 Mbps transfer rate in the 2.4 GHz frequency. (Some vendors, such as D-Link, have increased the rate on their devices to 22 Mbps.) It has a range up to 1,000 feet in an open area and 200 to 400 feet in an enclosed space (where walls might hamper the signal). It is backward compatible with 802.11, but is not interoperable with 802.11a.

802.11g

The specification for wireless data throughput at the rate of up to 54 Mbps in the 2.4 GHz band. It is compatible with 802.11b and may operate at a much faster speed.

802.11n

A recent specification for wireless data throughput with dramatic increased speeds and data throughput up to 600 Mbps in the 2.4 GHz or 5 GHz ranges.

802.11ac

A specification that improves on 802.11n by adding wider channels in the 5 GHz band to increase data throughput to a total of 1300 Mbps.

Wireless Security Protocols

Wired Equivalent Privacy (WEP)

Provides 64-bit, 128-bit and 256-bit encryption using the Rivest Cipher 4 (RC4) algorithm for wireless communication that uses the 802.11a and 802.11b protocols. WEP is deprecated because it relied on a 24-bit initialization vector (IV) to randomize identical strings of text, which made it vulnerable to an IV attack that could predict the IV value.

Wireless Transport Layer Security (WTLS)

The security layer of the Wireless Application Protocol (WAP) that uses public key cryptography for mutual authentication and data encryption. In most cases, WTLS is meant to provide secure WAP communications, but if it is improperly configured or implemented, it can expose wireless devices to attacks that include email forgery and sniffing data that has been sent in plaintext.

802.1x

An IEEE standard used to provide a port-based authentication mechanism over a LAN or wireless LAN. For wireless communications, 802.1x uses the 802.11a and 802.11b protocols. 802.1x also uses the Extensible Authentication Protocol (EAP) to provide user authentication against a directory service.

Wi-Fi Protected Access (WPA/WPA2)

The security protocol introduced to address some of the shortcomings in WEP. WPA was introduced during the development of the 802.11i IEEE standard and WPA2 implemented all the mandatory components of the standard. It provides for dynamic reassignment of keys to prevent the key-attack vulnerabilities of WEP:

- WPA provides improved data encryption through the Temporal Key Integrity Protocol (TKIP), which is a security protocol created by the IEEE 802.11i task group to replace WEP. It is combined with the existing WEP encryption to provide a 128-bit encryption key that fixes the key length issues of WEP.
- In addition to TKIP, WPA2 adds Advanced Encryption Standard (AES) cipher-based Counter Mode with Cipher Block Chaining Message Authentication Code Protocol (CCMP) encryption for even greater security and to replace TKIP. It provides a 128-bit encryption key.
- WEP regulates access to a wireless network based on a computer's hardware specific MAC address, which is relatively easy to figure out, steal and use (that is, sniff and spoof).

EAP

A framework that allows clients and servers to authenticate with each other using one of a variety of plug-ins. EAP does not specify which authentication method should be used and can be used in wireless and wired networks.

Two common EAP implementations are:

- Protected Extensible Authentication Protocol (PEAP), which is an open standard developed by a coalition made up of Cisco Systems, Microsoft and RSA Security.
- Lightweight Extensible Authentication Protocol (LEAP), which is Cisco Systems' proprietary EAP implementation.

WAP

Wireless Application Protocol (WAP) is a protocol designed to transmit data such as webpages, email and newsgroups postings to and from wireless devices such as mobile phones, smartphones and handheld computers over very long distances and display the data on small screens on a web-like interface.

WAP uses the proprietary Wireless Markup Language (WML) rather than native Hypertext Markup Language (HTML).

WAP has five layers:

1. Wireless Application Environment
2. Wireless Session Protocol
3. Wireless Transport Protocol
4. WTLS
5. Wireless Datagram Protocol

WAP was developed by companies such as Ericsson, Motorola and Nokia. The standard is currently maintained by the Open Mobile Alliance (OMA).

VPNs and Open Wireless

Open wireless networks are a major security risk when accessed directly. When using open wireless networks, you should tunnel through using a VPN, if feasible. VPNs provide authentication techniques and encrypt your data in transit over the Internet, even when using an insecure wireless hotspot. However, the VPN must use a secure tunneling protocol. E.g. Point-to-Point Tunneling Protocol (PPTP) is vulnerable to man-in-the-middle attacks; instead, you should use the more secure IPSec protocol when tunneling with a VPN.

Wireless Security Methods

Configuration

- Secure your wireless router or access point administration interface.
- Change default administrator passwords (and user names).
- Disable remote administration.
- Secure/disable the reset switch/function.
- Change the default SNMP parameter.
- Change the default channel.
- Regularly upgrade the Wi-Fi router firmware for the latest security patches and critical fixes.
- Implement MAC filtering.

Service Set Identifier (SSID)

- Don't broadcast your SSID.
- Change the default SSID broadcast

Encryption

- Enable WPA2 encryption instead of WEP.
- Change the default encryption keys.
- Avoid using pre-shared keys (PSK).

Network

- Assign static IP addresses to devices.
- Use the Remote Authentication Dial-In User Service Plus (RADIUS+) network directory authentication where feasible.
- Use a VPN.
- Perform periodic rogue wireless access point scans.
- Perform periodic security assessments.

Antenna placement and power level configuration

- Reduce your wireless LAN transmitter power.
- Position the router or access point safely. The radio frequency range of each access point should not extend beyond the physical boundaries of the organization's facilities.
- Adjust the power level controls on routers and access points as needed to help minimize power consumption within the wireless network, but to also provide the right level of power for operation.

Client

- Do not auto-connect to open Wi-Fi networks.
- Enable firewalls on each computer and the router.

Captive Portals

A captive portal is a technique that requires a client attempting to connect to the Internet to authenticate through a web page. Captive portals are commonly used by Wi-Fi hotspots, in order to get the user to agree to an acceptable use policy before they begin to use the service. They may also be used to authenticate users by requiring them to log in with the proper credentials, preventing unauthorized users from joining the network.

Site Surveys

In a general sense, a site survey is the collection of information on a location, including access routes, potential obstacles and best positioning of materials, for the purpose of constructing something in the best possible way. This is accomplished by modeling the environment using specialized tools that collect RF signal data.

Guidelines for Securing Wireless Traffic

When you secure wireless traffic, you must prevent unauthorized network access and the theft of network data while ensuring that authorized users can connect to the network.

- Keep sensitive data private. Do not include data you are not willing to lose if the wireless device is stolen or lost.
- Install antivirus software if it is available for your wireless device.
- Update the software to provide additional functionality and to close security holes such as:
  * prevent bluejacking and bluesnarfing attacks by disabling the discovery setting on Bluetooth connections.
  * set Bluetooth connections to hidden.
- Use a VPN with a strong tunneling protocol like IPSec when connecting to an insecure open wireless network.
- Conduct a site survey to determine the best possible ways to position your wireless infrastructure with respect to security.
- Implement a security protocol.
- Implement appropriate authentication and access control, such as RADIUS to prevent authentication attacks, including war driving.

- Implement an IDS on the wireless network for monitoring network activity to protect against rogue access point attacks and data emanation.
- Don't solely rely on MAC filtering and disabling SSID broadcasts.
- Implement a captive portal requiring login credentials to protect against unauthorized users accessing your Wi-Fi hotspot.
- Implement your hardware and software manufacturers' security recommendations.
- Test the functionality of systems after hardening them to make sure that required services and resources are accessible to legitimate users.
- Document your changes.

Chapter 5 - Implementing Access Control Authentication and Account Management

Access Control and Authentication Services

Strong authentication and access control are the first lines of defense in the battle to secure network resources.

Directory Services

A directory service is a network service that stores identity information about all the objects in a particular network, including users, groups, servers, clients, printers and network services. The directory also provides user access control to directory objects and network resources. Directory services can also be used to centralize security and to control access to individual network resources.

Directory Schema

The structure of the directory is controlled by a schema that defines rules for how objects are created and what their characteristics can be. Most schemas are extensible, so they can be modified to support the specific needs of an organization.

LDAP

The Lightweight Directory Access Protocol (LDAP) is a directory access protocol that runs over Transmission Control Protocol/Internet Protocol (TCP/IP) networks. LDAP clients authenticate to the LDAP service and the service's schema defines the tasks that clients can and cannot perform while accessing a directory database, the form the directory query must take and how the directory server will respond. The LDAP schema is extensible, which means you can make changes or add on to it.

Directory Management Tools

Most directory services are shipped with their own management tools. There are also a wide variety of third-party LDAP browsing and administration tools available for both open and closed source vendors.

In addition to preconfigured tools, you can create scripts that use LDAP to automate routine directory maintenance tasks, such as adding large numbers of users or groups and checking for blank passwords or disabled or obsolete user accounts.

LDAPS

Secure LDAP (LDAPS) is a method of implementing LDAP using Secure Sockets Layer/Transport Layer Security (SSL/TLS) encryption protocols to prevent eavesdropping and man-in-the-middle attacks. LDAPS forces both client and server to establish a secure connection before any transmissions can occur and if the secure connection is interrupted or dropped, LDAP likewise closes. The server implementing LDAPS requires a signed certificate issued by a certificate authority and the client must accept and install the certificate on their machine.

Common Directory Services

Microsoft® Active Directory®

A directory service that holds information about all network objects for a single domain or multiple domains. Active Directory allows administrators to centrally manage and control access to resources using Access Control Lists (ACLs). It allows users to find resources anywhere on the network. Active Directory also has a schema that controls how accounts are created and what attributes an administrator may assign to them. Active Directory Application Mode (ADAM) is a lightweight version of Active Directory.

Sun Java™ System Directory Server

This is the latest version of Sun Microsystems' Directory Server. It was formerly known as Sun ONE Directory Server and iPlanet Directory Server. Sun Java System Directory Server is built with 64-bit technology and marketed toward large installations that require reliable scaling. The software is free and paid support is available from Sun.

OpenDS

An open-source directory server that runs on Linux, Unix, Microsoft® Windows® and Mac OS X®. OpenDS is written by Sun in Java. It supports LDAPv3 and Directory Service Markup Language version 2 (DSMLv2).

OpenLDAP

A free, open-source LDAP implementation with distributions available for most operating systems.

Open Directory

Apple's customized implementation of OpenLDAP that is part of the Server app for Mac OS X. Open Directory is somewhat compatible with both Active Directory and Novell's eDirectory™ and integrates both the LDAP and Kerberos standards.

Directory Service Vulnerabilities

Common vulnerabilities to be aware of:

- All categories of network-based attacks, including:
  * Denial of Service (DoS)/Distributed Denial of Service (DDoS) attacks.
  * Unencrypted transmission of data.
  * Man-in-the-middle attacks.
  * Packet sniffing/capture attacks.
- Buffer overflow attacks.
- Security of user and administrator accounts and passwords.

Backing up Active Directory

You back up Active directory by backing up the computer's system state data within the Windows Backup utility. The following components are also backed up:

- Registry
- COM+ Class Registration database
- Boot and system files
- Certificate Services database (if you have installed Certificate Services on the server)

- The SYSVOL folder (if the server is a domain controller)
- The IIS Metabase (if you have installed IIS)

Remote Access Methods

Companies that require privacy may connect to a gateway remote access server (RAS) that provides access control services to all or part of the internal network. Also, an intermediate network – such as the Internet – can provide remote access from a remote system or a wireless device to a private network.

Tunneling

Tunneling is a data-transport technique that can be used to provide remote access in which a data packet is encrypted and encapsulated in another data packet in order to conceal the information of the packet inside. This enables data from one network to travel through another network. The tunnel can provide additional security by hiding user-encrypted data from the carrier network. Tunneling is typically employed as a security measure in VPN connections.

Remote Access Protocols

Point-to-Point Protocol (PPP)

This is a legacy Internet standard for sending IP datagram packets over serial point-to-point links. Its most common use is for dial-up Internet access. It can be used in synchronous and asynchronous connections. Point-to-Point Protocol over Ethernet (PPPoE) and Point-to-Point Protocol over ATM (PPPoA) are more recent PPP implementations used by many Digital Subscriber Line (DSL) broadband Internet connections.

PPP can dynamically configure and test remote network connections and is often used by clients to connect to networks and the Internet. It also provides encryption for passwords, paving the way for secure authentication of remote users.

Point-to-Point Tunneling Point (PPTP)

This is a Microsoft VPN Layer 2 protocol that increases the security of PPP by providing tunneling and data encryption for PPP packets. It uses the same authentication types as PPP and is a common VPN method among older Windows clients. PPTP encapsulates any type of network protocol and transports it over IP networks. However, because it has serious vulnerabilities, PPTP is no longer recommended by Microsoft.

Layer Two Tunneling Protocol (L2TP)

This is an Internet-standard protocol combination of PPTP and Layer 2 Forwarding (L2F) that enables the tunneling of PPP sessions across a variety of network protocols, such as IP. Frame Relay or Asynchronous Transfer Mode (ATM). L2TP was specifically designed to provide tunneling and security interoperability for client-to-gateway and gateway-to-gateway connections. L2TP does not provide any encryption on its own and L2TP tunnels appear as IP packets, so L2TP employs IP Security (IPSec) Transport Mode for authentication, integrity and confidentiality.

Secure Socket Tunneling Protocol (SSTP)

This protocol uses the Hypertext Transfer Protocol over Secure Sockets Layer (HTTP over SSL) protocol and encapsulates an IP packet with a PPP header and then with an SSTP header. The IP packet, PPP header and SSTP header are encrypted by the SSL session. An IP header containing the destination addresses is then added to the packet. It is supported in all current Windows operating systems.

HOTP

HMAC-based one-time password (HOTP) is an algorithm that generates one-time passwords (OTPs) using a hash-based message authentication code (HMAC) to ensure the authenticity of a message. One-time passwords are meant to replace insecure static passwords as an additional factor of authentication. The OTP is only valid for one particular session; after that, it will no longer be of use in access or authentication.

TOTP

Time HMAC-based one-time password (TOTP) improves upon the HOTP algorithm by introducing a time-based factor to the one-time password authentication. HOTP and other one-time passwords have a weakness that allows an attacker to take advantage of the password if it is never used. The temporary password is only invalidated after it is successfully used to authenticate, but if it never is, then it could stay active indefinitely. If an attacker gains access to an unused password they could easily compromise the system.

The TOTP algorithm addresses this security flaw by generating and invalidating new passwords in specific increments of time, such as 60 seconds.

PAP

Password Authentication Protocol (PAP) is an authentication protocol that sends user IDs and passwords as plaintext. It is generally used when a remote client is connecting to a non-Windows server that does not support strong password encryption. When the server receives a user ID and password pair, it compares them to its local list of credentials. If a match is found, the server accepts the credentials and allows the remote client to access resources. If no match is found, the connection is terminated. Because it lacks encryption, PAP is extremely vulnerable and has been largely phased out as a legacy protocol.

CHAP

Challenge Handshake Authentication Protocol (CHAP) is an encrypted authentication protocol that is often used to provide access control for remote access servers. CHAP was developed so that passwords would not have to be sent in plaintext. It is generally used to connect to non-Microsoft servers. CHAP uses a combination of Message Digest 5 (MD5) hashing and a challenge-response mechanism and it accomplishes authentication without ever sending passwords over the network. It can accept connections from any authentication method except for certain unencrypted schemes. For these reasons, CHAP is a more secure protocol than PAP. However, CHAP is also considered a legacy protocol, particularly because the MD5 hash algorithm is no longer suitably secure.

The CHAP Process

Step 1: The remote client requests a connection to the RAS.

Step 2: The remote server sends a challenge sequence, which is usually a random value.

Step 3: The remote client uses its password as an encryption key to encrypt the challenge sequence and sends the modified sequence to the server.

Step 4: The server encrypts the original challenge sequence with the password stored in its local credentials list and compares the results with the modified sequence received from the client:

- If the two sequences do not match, the server closes the connection.
- If the two sequences match, the server allows the client to access resources.

Guidelines for Securing Remote Access

To ensure that your users can connect remotely with an adequate layer of security to protect your systems:

- Set up a VPN for offsite employees to connect to your internal network through the Internet.
- Use secure tunneling protocols like L2TP with IPSec in your VPN.
- Avoid insecure tunneling protocols like PPTP.
- For those employees who access highly sensitive data, implement one-time password authentication.
- Implement time-based OTPs to mitigate the threat of a session being hijacked.
- Avoid using PAP and CHAP and other outdated remote access protocols that fail to provide adequate protection.

PGP

Privacy Good Privacy (PGP) is a publicly available email security and authentication utility that uses a variation of public key cryptography to encrypt emails: the sender encrypts the contents of the email message and then encrypts the key that was used to encrypt the contents. The encrypted key is sent with the email and the receiver decrypts the key and then uses the key to decrypt the contents. PGP also uses public key cryptography to digitally sign emails to authenticate the sender and the contents.

GPG

GNU Privacy Guard (GPG) is a free, open-source version of PGP that provides equivalent encryption and authentication services. GPG is compliant with current PGP services and meets the latest standards issued by the Internet Engineering Task Force (IETF).

RADIUS

Remote Authentication Dial-In User Service (RADIUS) is an Internet standard protocol that provides centralized remote access authentication, authorization and auditing services. When a network contains several remote access servers, you can configure one of the servers to be a RADIUS server and all of the other servers as RADIUS clients. The RADIUS clients will pass all authentication requests to the RADIUS server for verification. User configuration, remote access policies and usage logging can be centralized on the RADIUS server. In this configuration, the remote access server is generically known as the Network access Server (NAS).

Diameter

Diameter is an authentication protocol that improves upon RADIUS by strengthening some of its weaknesses. The name "Diameter" comes from the claim that Diameter is twice as good as RADIUS. Diameter is a stronger protocol in many ways but is not as widespread in its implementation due to the lack of products using it.

NPS

Network Policy Server (NPS) is a Microsoft Server 2012 implementation of a RADIUS server. It helps in administrating VPNs and wireless networks. NPS was known as Internet Authentication Service (IAS) in Windows Server 2003.

TACACS

The Terminal Access Controller Access Control System (TACACS) and TACACS Plus (TACACS+) protocols provide centralized authentication and authorization services for remote users. TACACS+ also supports multi-factor authentication. TACACS+ is considered more secure and more scalable than RADIUS because it accepts login requests and authenticates the access credentials of the user. TACACS+ includes process-wide encryption for authentication, whereas RADIUS encrypts only passwords. The original TACACS and another extension developed by Cisco, XTACACS, have been effectively replaced by the more secure TACACS+.

Kerberos

Kerberos is an authentication service that is based on a time-sensitive ticket-granting system. It was developed by the Massachusetts Institute of Technology (MIT) to use a single sign-on (SSO) method where the user enters access credentials that are then passed to the authentication server, which contains an access list and allowed access credentials. Kerberos can be used to manage access control to many different services using one centralized authentication server.

The Kerberos Process

In the Kerberos process:

1. A user logs on to the domain.
2. The user requests a ticket granting ticket (TGT) from the authenticating server.
3. The authenticating server responds with a time-stamped TGT.
4. The user presents the TGT back to the authenticating server and requests a service ticket to access a specific resource.
5. The authenticating server responds with a service ticket.

6. The user presents the service ticket to the resource.
7. The resource authenticates the user and allows access.

SAML

Security Assertion Markup Language (SAML) is a data format based on XML that is used to exchange authentication information between a service, an identity provider and the requesting client. SAML coordinates the various identity assertions between these three sources. Using XML as a framework, SAML defines security request information in markup language. This request information contains details such as when a request was issued, what resource is being requested and any conditions that need to be met. It efficiently implements web-based single sign-on authentication across many different protocols.

Implement Account Management Security Controls

Identity Management

Identity management is an area of information security that is used to identify individuals within a computer system or network. Identities are created with specific characteristics and information specific to each individual or resource in a system. Security professionals need to apply proper security controls to protect the identities of all individuals within a system and to prevent identity theft by unauthorized users. One aspect of identity management is

Account Management

Account management is a common term used to refer to the processes, functions and policies used to effectively manage user accounts within an organization. Account management job functions should follow the appropriate processes and security guidelines documented in an organizational security policy or account management policy. User accounts allow or deny access to an organization's information systems and resources; therefore, with the proper controls in place, organizations can properly manage accounts.

Account Privileges

Account privileges are permissions granted to users that allow them to perform various actions such as creating, deleting and editing files and also accessing systems and services on the network. Privileges can be assigned by user or by group. User assigned privileges are unique to each system user and can be configured to meet the needs of a specific job function or task. Group based privileges are assigned to an entire group of users within an organization. Each user within the group will have the same permissions applied.

User and group privileges should be well documented in an organization's account policy. A user who has unique user assigned privileges and who is also a member of a group will be granted both sets of privileges.

Account Policy

An account policy is a document that includes an organization's requirements for account creation, account monitoring and account removal. Policies can include user-specific guidelines or group management guidelines. It is necessary to research and analyze your organization's policy needs based on business requirements. Some policy statements include:

- Who can approve account creation?
- Who is allowed to use a resource?
- Whether or not users can share accounts or have multiple accounts.

- When and how an account should be disabled or modified after a user access review.
- When to enforce general account prohibition.
- What rules should be enforced for password history, password strength and password reuse.

Multiple Accounts

Multiple user accounts can occur when one individual has several accounts for a system or resource. Accounts may differ on the level of access applied, such as a user level account versus an administrator account. There are issues related to assigning and managing multiple accounts, such as:

- Lack of user awareness of the various accounts.
- Assigning the right level of data access and permissions to the appropriate accounts.
- Managing the privileges, permissions and data replication for each individual's accounts.

The management challenge is to enable the user to be able to access the elevated privileges of the administrative account when needed, without losing all the other environment settings that support productivity.

Shared Accounts

Shared accounts are accessed by more than one user or resource and unlike traditional unshared accounts, they are not associated with any one individual. Shared accounts are typically associated with a specific role or purpose that many users can share for a variety of reasons:

- Anonymous and guest accounts function as a way for visitors to access a system.
- Temporary accounts are useful for employees or contractors who work for a company inconsistently.

- Administrative accounts allow multiple authorized professionals access to higher privileges.
- Batch process accounts allow for easily automating many different types of tasks.

Shared accounts are an inherent security risk. Since many different people will use one account, it is extremely difficult – and often impossible – to hold specific individuals accountable in case of a breach. Likewise, the users themselves may recognize this and become careless with security, something they might avoid if they were logged in to their own personal accounts. The other major risk involves password changes to an account. Since frequent password changing is a common policy, organizations will need to ensure that everyone who has access to an account knows when the password will change and what the new password will be. This necessitates distributing passwords to a large group of people, which itself poses a significant challenge to security.

Account Federation

Account federation is the practice of linking a single account and its characteristics across many different account management systems. SSO is a subset of account federation that specifically works with authentication, where as account federation encompasses all of the policies and protocols that contribute to an identity. This provides a centralized account management structure that eliminates the need for superfluous account information. Federated accounts not only relieve some of the strain on the host, but users find that streamlining a single account for multiple use cases is much more practical and efficient than needing many different accounts. However, this also creates a single point of compromise for a user's identity. If the federated account's credentials are stolen, then an attacker can use that account in all of its different functions.

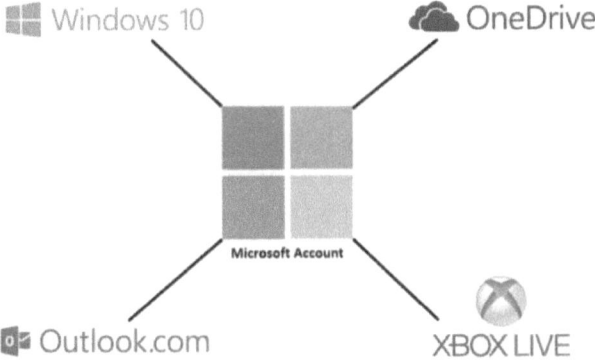

Account Management Security Controls

To maintain and enforce the security needs of an organization, strict account management security controls should be implemented and enforced.

User ID and password requirements

They should be managed and implemented with strict guidelines:

- They are required to access all data systems and services within a network or when accessing services on the Internet.
- Unique user IDs are required and documented for each system user.
- Strong, complex passwords are required and documented for every system user, along with the character length requirements.
- Password and user account recovery procedures should be documented and followed by administrators.
- Passwords should change often and reusing the same passwords should not be allowed.

Account access restrictions

Account access guidelines should be documented for each type of account used within an organization. E.g. user account and group account privileges and system access information should be documented. The concept of least privilege should be used when granting or denying access.

Account management guidelines

Account management can include a number of different tasks. The most common security guidelines include account creation, disablement, lockout and expiration. Security guidelines should include organizational procedures for each account action and what specific conditions must be present to allow for an account change or deletion.

Multiple account guidelines

- Ensure proper documentation of all accounts assigned to an individual, including privileges, permissions and data access rights assigned to each type of account.
- Verify that user accounts are assigned properly and that each individual has only the necessary accounts assigned to perform his or her job.
- Verify that the proper level of access is assigned to each account.

Continuous monitoring

Account management should be considered an ongoing practice with regard o security. Monitoring various events like successful and failed logon attempts, escalation of rights and privileges and assigning new users and groups will help you zero in on any account abuse.

Credential Management

Credential managers were created to help users and organizations more easily store and organize account user names and passwords. These applications typically store credentials in an encrypted database on the local machine. From there, an authenticated user can retrieve the proper credentials for the relevant system.

Credential managers are only as strong as the password they store. If the database of passwords is encrypted by a master key, then the attacker who discovers it shall compromise the entire credential database. Using multi-factor authentication increases security.

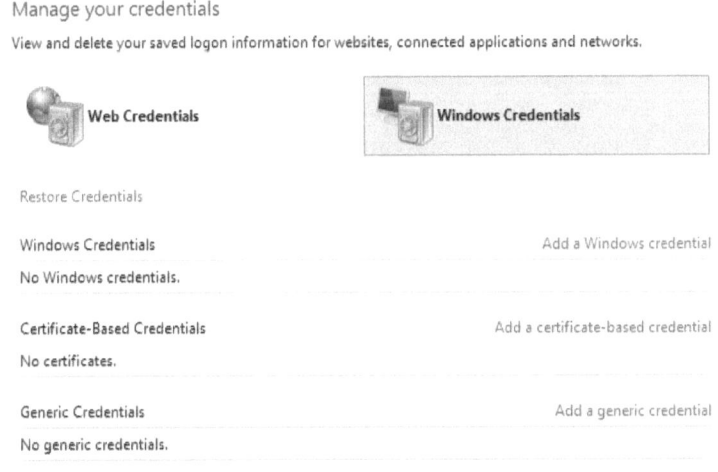

Manage your credentials

View and delete your saved logon information for websites, connected applications and networks.

Group Policy

The Group Policy service in Windows systems provides several different methods for managing account security across a domain. Examples include:

- Enforcing account password properties like length, complexity and age.

- Enforcing account lockout thresholds and durations.
- Storing account passwords using reversible encryption.
- Enforcing Kerberos logon restrictions and ticket lifetimes.
- Auditing account management events.
- Assigning specific rights and controls to individual or group accounts.

Guidelines for Implementing Account Management Security Controls

With proper account management security controls in place, you can ensure that the identity and logon information for all individuals within an organization is fully protected from unauthorized access or theft.

- Impalement the principle of least privilege when assigning user and group account access.
- Ensure that an account policy exists and includes all account policy guidelines.
- Verify that account request and approval procedures exist and are enforced.
- Verify that account modification procedures exist and are enforced.
- Verify that strong user name and password guidelines exist and are documented.
- Verify that account usage guidelines exist and are documented, such as how to manage inactive accounts
- Limit the use of multiple and shared accounts to protect them from abuse.
- Store user names and passwords in encrypted databases with credentialed management software.
- Implement a group policy for wider access control.
- Continuously monitor account events such as logons and privilege escalation.

Chapter 6 - Managing

Certificates

Install a CA Hierarchy

You can implement certificate-based security either by obtaining certificates from a public Certificate Authority (CA) or by establishing your own CA.

Digital Certificates

A digital certificate is an electronic document that associates credentials with a public key. Both users and devices can hold certificates. The certificate validates the certificate holder's identity and is also a way to distribute the holder's public key. A server called a Certificate Authority (CA) issues certificates and the associated public/private key pairs.

Certificate Authentication

When a user authenticates using a certificate, the user presents a digital certificate in place of a user name and password. A user is authenticated if the certificate is validated by a CA.

Certificate authentication is therefore the process of identifying end users in a transaction that involves a series of steps to be carried out before the user's identity is confirmed. These can include initiating a secure transaction, such as a client requesting access to a secure site. The secure site presents its digital certificate to the client, enclosing its public key and verified digital signature. The client browser validates the signature against its cache of trusted and acknowledged certificates, comparing it to a library of CAs.

Once the digital signature is accepted, certificate authentication is successful. If the issuing CA does not match one in the library of CAs, then certificate authentication is unsuccessful and the user obtains a notification that the digital certificate supplied is invalid.

PKI

A Public Key Infrastructure (PKI) is a system that is composed of a CA, certificates, software, services and other cryptographic components, for the purpose of enabling authenticity and validation of data and entities. The PKI can be implemented in various hierarchical structures and can be publicly available or maintained privately by an organization. A PKI can be used to secure transactions over the Internet.

PKI Components

A PKI contains several components:

- Digital certificates, to verify the identity of entities,
- One or more CAs, to issue digital certificates to computers, users or applications.
- A Registration Authority (RA), responsible for verifying users' identities and approving or denying requests for digital certificates.
- A certificate repository database, to store the digital certificates.
- A certificate management system, to provide software tools to perform the day-to-day functions of the PKI.
- A certificate signing request (CSR), a message sent to a CA in which a resource applies for a certificate.

PKCS

Public Key Cryptography Standards (PKCS) is the most common CSR format, developed by a consortium of vendors to send information over the Internet in a secure manner using a PKI. Important PKCS standards include:

- **PKCS #7 – Cryptographic Message Syntax standard:** A PKCS that describes the general syntax used for cryptographic data, such as digital signatures.
- **PKCS #10 – Certification Request Syntax Standard:** A PKCS that describes the syntax used to request certification of a public key and other information.

CA Hierarchies (Trust Models)

A CA hierarchy or trust model is a single CA or group of CAs that work together to issue digital certificates. Each CA in the hierarchy has a parent-child relationship with the CA directly above it. A CA hierarchy provides a way for multiple CAs to distribute the certificate workload and provide certificate services more efficiently. If a CA is compromised, only those certificates issued by that particular CA and its children are invalid. The remaining CAs in the hierarchy will continue to function.

The Root CA

The root CA is he topmost CA in the hierarchy and consequently the most trusted authority. The root CA issues and self-signs the first certificate in the hierarchy. The root CA must be secured, because if it is compromised all other certificates become invalid.

Microsoft® CA Terminology

If a Microsoft® CA is integrated with Active Directory®, it is called an enterprise CA; if not, it is considered a standalone CA.

Public and Private Roots

Root CAs can be designated as either public or private:

- A private root CA is created by a company for use primarily within the company itself. The root can be set up and configured in-house or contracted to a third-party vendor.
- A public root CA is created by a third-party or commercial vendor for general access by the public.

Commercial CAs

VeriSign® is a well-known provider of public certificate services, along with Comodo™, GlobalSign® and Entrust®.

Subordinate CAs

Subordinate CAs are any CAs below the root in the hierarchy. Subordinate CAs issue certificates and provide day-to-day management of the certificates, including renewal, suspension and revocation.

Offline Root CAs

To provide the most secure environment possible for the root CA, companies will often set up the root CA and then take it offline, allowing the subordinate CAs to issue all certificates. The root CA remains offline and is not patched again once it is taken offline. All updates are installed physically on all subordinate CAs. This strategy ensures that the root CA is not accessible by anyone on the network and thus, it is much less likely to be compromised.

CA Hierarchy Design Opinions

The design of your CA hierarchy will depend on your organization's business and security requirements.

Thousands of employees worldwide: The subordinate CAs are designated by geographic location to balance the number of issued certificates among the individual CAs.

Individuals need to access specific applications only: The subordinate CAs are designated by function or department so the individual CAs serve groups of people with specific resource needs.

Tight security allows individuals to have differing levels of access to the same resources: The subordinate CAs are designated by the security required to obtain a certificate. Some CAs may be set up to issue a certificate with a network ID and password; other CAs may require a person to present a valid driver's license.

Enroll Certificates

The Certificate Enrollment Process

Users and other entities obtain certificates from the CA through the certificate enrollment process.

1. **Entity requests certificate:** An entity follows the procedure (e.g. filling out an online form) to obtain a certificate.

2. **RA authenticates entity:** Authentication is determined by the certificate policy requirements (e.g. a network user ID and password, driver's license or other unique identifier).

3. **Policy applied to request:** The RA applies the certificate policy that pertains to the particular CA that will issue the certificate.

4. **Request sent to CA:** If the identity of the entity is authenticated successfully and the policy requirements are met, the RA sends the certificate request on to the CA.

5. **CA issues certificate:** The CA creates the certificate and puts it in the repository.

6. **Entity notified:** The CA notifies the entity that the certificate is available and the certificate is delivered.

7. **Certificate installed:** Once the certificate is obtained, it can be installed using the appropriate tool.

The Certificate Life Cycle

1. **Issuance:** The life cycle begins when the root CA has issued its self-signed key pair. The root CA then begins issuing certificates to other CAs and end users.

2. **Enrollment:** Users and other entities obtain certificates from the CA through certificate enrollment.

3a. **Renewal:** Certificates can be renewed more than once depending on the certificate policy parameters.

3b. **Revocation:** Certificates can be revoked before their expiration date, which renders them permanently invalid. Certificates can be revoked for a variety of reasons, including misuse, loss or compromise.

3c. **Expiration:** Certificates expire after a given length of time, which is established in the certificate policy and configured in the issuing CA. The expiration parameter is part of the certificate data. If the root CA's certificate expires, the entire CA becomes inactive.

3d. Suspension: Some CAs support temporary suspension of certificates, in addition to permanent revocation.

Certificate Life Cycle Management

As a general rule, the longer the life cycle is, the less administrative overhead is involved. However, this could pose a higher security risk, because a longer life cycle also gives attackers more time to break the cryptography of the key pair or otherwise compromise the system. Also, with a shortened lifetime, new developments in cryptography could allow you to have entities renew certificates that are more secure. The actual life cycle of your certificates will be based on your business requirements and security needs.

Balancing Certificate Life Cycle Needs

Although it would seem that a long key pair combined with a very complex algorithm would provide the longest life cycle and less administrative overhead, this combination can increase the time it takes to encrypt and decrypt data on the network. A long life cycle also allows attackers more time to break the code. You must balance the needs for security and accessibility when you design your certificate hierarchy.

Certificate Life Cycle Factors

Length of the private key

The longer the key, the more data bits there are to work with. Long keys require more resources (more central processing unit [CPU] cycles or memory, more computers, more time and so on) to break. Attackers may not think it is worth the effort.

Strength of the cryptography used

The more complex the mathematical functions are that are used in the algorithm, the harder it is for an attacker to decrypt. But it means that the time taken to generate the keys will also be higher.

Physical security of the CA and private key

Higher physical security is essential for longer life cycles. All the policies in the world will not protect a private key if it is not physically secure. Keep in mind that physical security may be expensive.

Security of issued certificates and their private keys

The more secure the user's private keys are, the better they are for the security of the overall system. Conversely, users can forget passwords or lose smart cards and that means more work for administrators.

Risk of attack

Your CA may be secure, but an attacker can use another access point that is not as secure on your network to gain access to the CA.

User trust

You can generally trust internal users (employees on the corporate network) more than external users (individuals accessing through the Internet).

Although a long life cycle requires less administrative work (renewals, revocations and so on), it also gives attackers more time to gain access. This makes it important for administrators to keep track of certificate issues.

Secure Network Traffic by Using Certificates

Once an entity has a certificate enrolled, you can use the certificate to secure network traffic flowing to and from that entity.

The SSL Enrollment Process

You can use certificates to implement Secure Sockets Layer (SSL).

1. Request: The client requests a session with the server.
2. Response: The server responds by sending its digital certificate and public key to the client.
3. Negotiation: The server and client then negotiate an encryption level.
4. Encryption: Once they agree on an encryption level, the client generates a session key, encrypts it and sends it with the public key from the server.
5. Communication: The session key then becomes the key used in the conversation.

Renew Certificates

Because certificates are temporary and can expire, your first concern in maintaining them over their life cycle will be renewing the existing certificates at appropriate intervals.

Certificate Renewal

If certificates did not expire, an entity on the network could use one indefinitely even if its job role or function had changed. You should renew certificates appropriately so that you do not have any interruptions in your security services.

Back Up and Restore Certificates and Private Keys

Private Key Protection Methods

Private keys are crucial to the security of a CA hierarchy and must be protected from loss, theft or compromise. To secure a private key:

- Back it up to removable media and store the media securely.
- Delete it from insecure media.
- Require a password to restore the private key.
- Never share a key.
- Never transmit a key on the network or across the Internet after it is issued.
- Consider using key escrow to store a private key with trusted third parties.

Key Escrow

Key escrow, an alternative to key backups, can be used to store private keys securely, while allowing one or more trusted third parties access to the keys under predefined conditions. The third party is called the key escrow agent. For example, in certain situations, a government agency might require private keys to be placed in escrow with the agency. Commercial CAs can also act as escrow agents on a contract basis for organizations that do not want to back up and manage their own private keys.

M of N Control

In a key escrow scheme, there are only a certain number of agents or trustees that have the authority to recover a key. To prevent a single authorized agent from recovering a key, the M of N scheme is commonly used. The M of N scheme is a mathematical control that takes into account the total number of key recovery agents (N) along with the number of agents required to perform a key recovery (M). If the number of agents attempting to recover a key does not meet or exceed M, then the key will not be recovered. The exact values of M and N will vary with the implementation.

Private Key Restoration Methods

In the event that a private key is lost or damaged, you must restore the key from a backup or from escrow before you can recover any encrypted data.

- If you are using key escrow, the key is divided among escrow agents. The agents can use the parts to reconstruct the lost key or decrypt the information directly.
- If the key has been backed up to removable media, it can be restored from the backup location.

The (EFS) Recovery Agent

The Encrypting File System (EFS) uses Microsoft Windows NTFS-based public key encryption. Windows Server 2012 R2 automatically creates encryption certificates and public keys based on a user's credentials; or, you can use Windows Server 2012 R2's Active Directory Certificate Services (AD CS) to distribute certificate and keys.

File encryption keys, which are used to encrypt the files are stored by the public key. The files are then accessible only by using the file owner's private key. The file encryption keys are then stored in the Windows operating system kernel and are never copied to the paging file, thus providing another level of security. This, however, will not protect against damage to the operating system or server itself.

Windows Server 2012 R2 enables you to define an EFS recovery agent, in the event the user account which files are encrypted no longer exists. Perhaps it was deleted when the user left the organization. A recovery agent is an individual who has necessary credentials to recover files that were encrypted by another user. By default, Windows Server 2012 R2 designates the domain administrator as an EPS recovery agent.

Key Archival and Recovery

You can use AD CS to archive private keys in the protected CA database, which enables the private keys to be recovered. Key recovery does not recover encrypted data or messages, but it enables a user or administrator to recover keys that can subsequently be used for data recovery (or data decryption).

Private Key Replacement

If a private key is lost, you might wish to replace the key entirely after you recover any encrypted data:

1. First, recover the private key.
2. Decrypt any encrypted data.
3. Destroy the original private key.
4. Obtain a new key pair.
5. Finally, re-encrypt the data using the new private key.

Revoke Certificates

Certificate Revocation

Certificates can be revoked before expiration for one of several reasons:

- The certificate owner's private key has been compromised or lost.
- The certificate was obtained by fraudulent means.
- The certificate holder is no longer trusted. This can occur in normal circumstances, such as when an employee leaves a company, or it can be due to a system intrusion, such as when a subordinate CA is attacked.

Compromised CA

One example of a CA that is no longer trusted is the former certificate authority called DigiNotar. In 2011, the Dutch government revealed that DigiNotar was hacked and that the hackers granted at least 500 fraudulent certificates for agencies such as the CIA and England's MI6. The Dutch government then took action to shut down the compromised CA and many of its certificates were revoked.

The CRL

A Certificate Revocation List (CRL) is a list of certificates that were revoked before the expiration date. Each CA has its own CRL that can be accessed through the directory services of the network operating system or a website. The CRL generally contains the requester's name, the request ID number, the reason why the certificate was revoked and other pertinent information.

CRL Checked by Software

Many software programs, such as email applications, will check the CRL for the status of a certificate before accepting it and will reject revoked certificates.

Status Checking and Suspensions

In certificate systems that support temporary certificate suspensions as well as permanent certificate revocations, the certificate clients will check for both suspended and revoked certificates and will reject certificates that have been either suspended or revoked.

OCSP

The Online Certificate Status Protocol (OCSP) is an HTTP-based alternative to a CRL for checking the status of revoked certificates. OCSP servers, also called responders, accept a request to check a specific certificate's status. The responder uses the certificate's serial number to search for it in the CA's database. The server then sends the certificate's status to the requester.

The main advantage of using OCSP over a CRL is that it lowers overhead because OCSP responses for specific requests contain less data than entire revocation lists, which benefits both the client and network. However, because OCSP does not encrypt these standard HTTP transmissions, an attacker may glean that a network resource used a specific certificate at a specific time during this OCSP transaction.

Chapter 7 - Implementing

Compliance and

Operational Security

Physical Security

Physical Security Controls

Physical security controls are security measures that restrict, detect and monitor access to specific physical areas or assets.

There are various ways to categorize the different physical security controls:

- Deterrent controls discourage attackers from attacking in the first place.
- Preventive controls stop an attack before it can cause damage.
- Compensating controls support other physical controls.

- Technical controls are hardware or software that aid in protecting physical assets.
- Administrative controls leverage security policies and are used to train personnel.

Physical Security Control Types

Locks

Locks are used to prevent unauthorized access to information resources. They include:

- Bolting door locks
- Combination door locks or cipher locks
- Electronic door locks
- Biometric door locks
- Hardware locks

Logging and visitor access

Logging should be used at all entrances that are open to the general public. Visitors should sign in and out when entering and leaving the building. Logging requirements should include:

- Name of the company being represented.
- Date, time of entry and time of departure.
- Reason for visiting.
- Contact within the organization.

When possible, one single entry point should be used for all incoming visitors. This decreases the risk of unauthorized individuals gaining access to the building.

Identification systems

Security cards, such as swipe cards or proximity cards, provide identity information about the bearer, which is then checked against an appropriate access list for that location. The cards can be used along with a proximity reader to verify identification and grant access. A security cards can also include a picture or some other identification code for a second authentication factor. Security cards should be required for all employees and should be visible at all times.

Video surveillance

Video or still-image surveillance from closed-circuit television (CCTV) cameras can be put in place to deter or detect unwanted access. These systems can be placed inside and outside the building. All video recording should be saved and stored in a secure environment.

Security guards

Human security guards, armed or unarmed, can be placed in front of and around a location to protect it. They can monitor critical checkpoints and verify identification, allow or disallow access and log physical entry occurrences. They also provide a visual deterrent and can apply their own knowledge and intuition to potential security breaches.

Signs

Signs are simple and rudimentary, but they nevertheless can be effective against less determined intruders. Beyond basic no trespassing signs, some homes and offices also display signs from the security companies whose services they are currently using. These may convince intruders to stay away.

Bonded personnel

Contracted services personnel, such as cleaning services, should be bonded to protect an organization from financial exposures.

Mantrap doors

A mantrap door system, also referred to as a deadman door, is a system with a door at each end of a secure chamber. An individual enters a secure area through an outer door. The outer door must be closed before an inner door can open. An individual's identity is sometimes verified before they enter the secure area through the first door and other times while they are confined to the secure area between the two doors. This system also requires that one person enters at a time.

This system typically requires two separate authentication processes, with the second one being done while the authenticated person is isolated inside a reinforced enclosure.

Physical barriers

The location of highly secure resources, such as a server room, should not have windows or be visible from the outside of a building. This creates a more secure barrier from the outside. Examples of physical barriers include fencing, barricades and true floor-to-ceiling wall architectures.

Alarms

Alarms activated by an unauthorized access attempt require a quick response. Locally stationed security guards or police may respond to alarms. These responding individuals may trigger access control devices in the facility to automatically lock.

Motion detection

Sensors that detect motion may trip alarms and alert the authorities to a possible intruder. These sensors can be placed at checkpoints within or outside a building.

Protected distribution

Protected distribution systems are intended to make it difficult for attackers to compromise the physical cabling of a communications network. This is generally achieved by hardening the cables with strong metallic tubing and installing acoustic alarm systems that detect when the cabling is being tampered with. Additionally, protected distribution systems are routinely inspected by qualified personnel for any intrusions that the alarms did not catch.

Environmental Exposures

Environmental exposures must be considered when evaluating the overall security of a building. Exposures can include lightning, hurricanes, earthquakes, volcanic eruptions, high winds and other extreme weather conditions. As a result of any of these exposures, a number of issues may arise:

- Power fluctuation and failures.
- Water damage and flooding.
- Fires.
- Structural damage to the building leading to unauthorized access.

Environmental Controls

There are certain environmental controls that can be implemented to help control a facility's physical environment.

An HVAC system controls the environment inside a building.

- Humidity and temperature control: Most experts recommend that temperatures in a computer facility should be in the range 72° - 76° Fahrenheit. High and low temperatures can damage equipment. Low humidity causes static electricity, which can damage the sensitive circuitry of electronics; high humidity causes moisture buildup, which can lead to corrosion.

- Positive air pressure is a must. Air should be forced from the facility to keep contaminants out. Filters on HVAC systems keep dust to a minimum and must be changed regularly.

- To ensure that HVAC systems are running properly, it is important to monitor them both locally and remotely.

Hot and cold aisle

A method used within data centers and computer rooms to control the temperature and humidity. A hot and cold aisle layout is designed to control the flow of air to or from systems using strategically placed vents and exhaust fans to keep the hardware and room at the desired temperature and humidity.

Electromagnetic interference (EMI) shielding

EMI occurs when a magnetic field builds up around one electrical circuit and interferes with the signal being carried on an adjacent circuit, causing network interference issues resulting in signal noise or errors. EMI shielding is used to prevent electromagnetic transfers from cables and devices by creating a conductive material protective barrier. For example, a shielded cable contains an electromagnetic covering within the cable that directly protects the inner core conductor from producing an electromagnetic discharge.

Alarm control panel

The main control panel for an organization's alarm system should be protected and secured from any type of exposure. The panel must be in a separate location and protected from unauthorized access and be accessible by the fire department, encased in a waterproof and climate-controlled box, powered by a dedicated circuit and programmed to function by zone within an organization.

Fire prevention

The first rule of fire protection is fire prevention. Fires can be prevented by:

- Eliminating unnecessary storage items and clutter.
- Conducting annual inspections by the fire department, which include an extensive review of computer room controls, all fire suppression systems and extinguishers within the building.
- Installing fireproof walls and a fireproof floor and ceiling in the computer room, which all have at least two-hour fire resistance rating.
- Using fire-resistant office materials, such as garbage bins, desks, chairs and window treatments.

Fire detection

Commercial fire detection systems should be connected to a central reporting station where the location of the suspected fire is indicated. In some cases, the detection system or monitoring station is connected directly to a fire department. Various fire detection systems are used to identify the threat of a fire:

- Smoke detectors sense the presence of smoke using various scientific methods, such as testing for particles in the air.
- Heat sensors are triggered either when a target temperature is reached or when there is a high rate of increase in temperature.
- Flame detectors use optical sensors to record incoming radiation at selected wavelengths.

Fire suppression

Fires in computer facilities are especially dangerous. The damage done to computing systems is extremely expensive and the chemicals used in the machines may emit toxic substances during fires. In some cases, small fires may be extinguished using hand-held fire extinguishers. These systems must be placed in the appropriate locations within a facility and should be inspected regularly. When it is not practical to fight these fires with small extinguishers or to douse fires with water, then special gases should be used to extinguish fires in areas with a large number of computers or servers.

Frequently, local jurisdictions mandate water-based fire extinguishing systems, even though gaseous systems often provide more appropriate protection for computer equipment. To satisfy each requirement, organizations are outfitted with both. If the gas system does not suppress the fire, the sprinkler system will then activate, but is otherwise maintained as the official back-up extinguisher. The best practice is to contact your local fire authorities when designing a fire suppression system.

Environmental Monitoring

Regularly monitoring the environmental conditions and controls surrounding a building and the hardware stored inside it is important to properly secure and prevent damage to resources. Conditions that can threaten security should be monitored regularly, along with the implementation of necessary security controls. In some instances, constant video monitoring is used to look for environmental issues such as overheating, water or electricity issues.

Safety

The safety of your employees and your property are important concerns from a security standpoint. The health of your personnel and the hardware they work with is vital to keeping your operation running at maximum efficiency.

For example, physical controls like fencing and CCTV cameras will deter intruders and keep them from harming your assets. Locks may be placed on doors to hazardous areas, like a warehouse in which heavy machinery is used, in order to protect employees. Proper lighting during the night will keep late workers safe from accidents that occur as a result of poor visibility. For environmental hazards like fire or noxious gas, you need to formulate an escape plan. What is the best way to get all of your personnel out of the building as quickly and calmly as possible? You'll also need to map out the best escape routes in the event of an unsafe situation. However, no amount of written policy will be able to adequately prepare your personnel for such an event, so you should test their preparedness by performing drills.

The wear and tear that safety controls are subject to should be a primary concern. You need to make sure that there is no point in time when your personnel and property are left vulnerable. This is why you need to implement testing controls to consistently test your fencing, lighting, locks, CCTV cameras, escape plans etc. If any one of these controls does not meet your standards for safety, you will be able to quickly fix or replace it.

Compliance Laws and Regulations

Compliance is the practice of ensuring that the requirements of legislation, regulations, industry codes and standards and organizational standards are met. Several controlling authorities need to be recognized to achieve compliance:

- Governmental legislative entities such as national congresses or parliaments and state, provincial or regional senates or other law-making bodies.
- Governmental regulatory agencies that promulgate rules, regulations and standards for various industries.
- Industry associations that promulgate rules, regulations and standards for individual industries.

The effect of laws and regulations on applying security measures can be substantial. Security professionals must review all laws and regulations relevant to the type of business and operation that needs to be secured. Most organizations will have legal requirements that apply to their data systems, processes, controls and infrastructure. Regulations can affect the way businesses store, transmit and process data. When securing an organization as a whole, you must review the business' privacy policy and other legal documents that convey business requirements.

Legal Requirements

All organizations must consider their overall or general legal obligations, rights, liabilities and limitations when creating security policies. Because security incidents can potentially be prosecuted as technology crimes, organizations must be prepared to work with civil authorities when investigating, reporting and resolving each incident. Information security practices must comply with legal requirements that are documented in other departmental policies, such as human resources. A company's response to a security incident must conform to the company's legal limitations as well as the civil rights of the individuals involved.

In addition to the various local, state, federal and international legal considerations, organizations in regulated industries, such as utility companies, hazardous material manufacturers and medical professions, will have to comply with the additional standards and requirements imposed by governmental authorities and professions, will have to comply with the additional standards and requirements imposed by governmental authorities and professional oversight bodies for each industry. The requirements can vary widely, depending on the industry involved and are specific for every organization.

When applying security measures to an organization, it is always a good idea to consider industry best practices. Depending on the type of business, best practices will vary.

Types of Legal Requirements

Legal issues can affect different parties within each organization.

Employees

- Who is liable for the misuse of email and Internet resources? The organization, the employee, or both?
- What is the extent of liability for an organization for criminal acts committed by its employees?
- What rights to privacy do employees have regarding electronic communications?

Customers

- What customer data is considered private and what is considered public?
- How will a company protect the privacy and confidentiality of customer information?

Business partners

- Who is liable if data resides in one location (country) and the processing takes place in another location?
- Who is responsible for the security and privacy of the information transmitted between an organization and a business partner? The sender or the receiver?

Forensic Requirements

Information security professionals must observe generally accepted forensic practices when investigating security incidents.

Evidence collection

Following the correct procedures for collecting evidence from floppy disks, hard drives, smart cards and other media ensures the integrity of the evidence and prevents tampering. As in any other case, evidence that is improperly collected may not be admissible in court.

Evidence preservation

Criminal cases or even internal security incidents can take months or years to resolve. The company must be able to properly preserve all gathered evidence for a lengthy period of time.

Chain of custody

Whoever gathers and preserves the evidence must also maintain a complete inventory that shows who handled specific items and where they have been stored. This document must be kept secure at all times to prevent tampering. If the chain of custody is broken, it can be difficult, if not impossible, to prosecute a technology crime.

Jurisdiction

Determining exactly who has the right to investigate and prosecute an information technology criminal case can be extremely difficult due to overlapping laws for copyright, compute fraud and mail tampering. In addition, each country has its own laws and these laws may vary depending on what part of the country is involved. Organizations are obliged to use due care to determine the appropriate jurisdiction for a security investigation.

Security Awareness and Training

Security Policy Awareness

An organization's security policy is created to ensure that all system users comply with the security guidelines and procedures enforced by management. Security professionals should verify that the security policy is accessible and that users are trained in the importance of security awareness within an organization. Regular training sessions and security policy documentation will ensure that users follow the correct procedures when accessing and using system resources and services.

Role-Based Training

Training may be implemented based on job roles and organizational responsibilities. For instance, end users might not need training about how to keep budget or personal information secure, while managers would need to know the restrictions of sharing such data.

Role-based training may be technical or relating to incident reporting and response.

Personally Identifiable Information (PII)

Personally identifiable information (PII) is information that can be used on its own or with other information to identify, contact or locate a single person, or to identify an individual in context. What constitutes PII will vary depending on the legal jurisdiction. PII can include a user's full name, fingerprints, license plate number, phone numbers, street address, driver's license number and so on.

Classification of Information

To protect information from disclosure and other threats, the risk associated with the release or modification should be measured by labeling the information. Labeling schemes are known as classifications. The classifications depend on the type of business and how the data is stored. Classified data can be either hard or soft. Hard data refers to concrete information, such as measurements and facts about an organization. Soft data refers to the organization's ideas, thoughts and views. All data should be classified and protected accordingly.

Common information classifications include schemes where information is categorized according to the level of sensitivity in the information, such as:

- High, Medium and Low
- Restricted, Private and Public
- Confidential, Restricted and Public

Information that should not be provided to individuals outside of the enterprise.

Personal and confidential

Information of a personal nature that should be protected.

Private

Correspondence of a private nature between two people that should be safeguarded.

Trade Secret

Corporate intellectual property that, if released, will present serious damage to the company's ability to protect patens and processes.

Client Confidential

- Client personal information that, if released, may result in the identity theft of the individual.
- Client corporate information or intellectual property. You may need to sign a non-disclosure agreement (NDA) to keep an organization's information about a client confidential.

Employee Education

A comprehensive security plan can only succeed when all members of an organization understand the necessary security practices and comply with them. Security professionals are often the ones responsible for educating employees and encouraging their compliance with security policies.

Awareness

Employees must understand the importance of information security and security policies and have an awareness of the potential threats to security. Threats can include new and upcoming viruses, types of phishing attacks and zero day exploits.

Employees also need to be aware of the role they play to protect an organization's assets and resources. A security professional can create awareness through seminars, email or information on a company intranet.

Communication

The lines of communication between employees and the security team must remain open. Security professionals can accomplish this by encouraging employees to ask questions and provide feedback on security issues. Also, the security team must take responsibility for keeping the workforce informed of ongoing security concerns and updated best practices and standards.

Education

Employees should be trained and educated in security procedures, practices and expectations from the moment they walk through the door. Employees are responsible for organizational security the second they join an organization and have access to the physical building and resources and the intellectual property inside. Education should continue as technology changes and new information becomes available. Education takes many forms, from training sessions to online courses employees can take at work.

Educated users are one of your best defenses against social engineering attacks.

Online Resources

Providing employees with online access to security-related resources and information promotes employee awareness and training. You can provide proprietary, private security information, such as your corporate security policy document, through an organization's intranet. You can also point employees to a number of reputable and valuable security resources on the Internet. However, just because information is posted on a website does not mean it is factual or reliable.

Periodically monitor the websites you recommend to your employees to make sure that they are providing worthwhile information and encourage employees to verify any technical or security-related information with a reliable third party before acting on the information or passing it along to others.

Listed below are some of the information security resources that you can find on the Internet:

www.microsoft.com/security/default.mspx

/www.oracle.com/technetwork/topics/security/whatsnew/index.html

http://tools.cisco.com/security/center/home.x

www.sans.org

www.openssh.org

www.emc.com/domains/rsa/index.htm

/www.cert.org

searchsecurity.techtarget.com/

www.securityfocus.com

www.entrust.com

www.ruskwig.com

www.symantec.com/security_response/index.jsp

www.mcafee.com

http://project.honeynet.org

http://web.mit.edu/kerberos

http://hoaxbusters.org

http://vmyths.com

http://snopes.com

User Security Responsibilities

Because security is most often breached at the end-user level, users need to be aware of their specific security responsibilities and habits.

Physical security

Employees should not allow anyone in the building without an ID badge.

Employees should not allow other individuals to tailgate on a single ID badge.

Employees should be comfortable approaching and challenging unknown or unidentified persons in a work area. Access within the building should be restricted to only those areas an employee needs to access for job purposes. Data handling procedures of confidential files must be followed.

Employees must also follow clean desk policies to ensure that confidential documents and private corporate information are secured and filed away from plain sight.

System security

Proper password behaviors can be crucial in keeping systems resources secure from unauthorized users. Employees must use their user IDs and passwords properly and comply with the ID and password requirements set forth by management. Password information should never be shared or written down where it is accessible to others. All confidential files should be saved to an appropriate location on the network where they can be secured and backed up, not on a hard drive or removable media device.

Device security

Employees must use correct procedures to log off all systems and shut down computers when not in use. Wireless communication and personally owned devices must be approved by the IT department and installed properly. These devices can be a gateway for attackers to access corporate information and sensitive data. Portable devices, such as laptops and mobile devices, must be properly stored and secured when not in use.

Social networking security

Employees must be made aware of the potential threats and attacks that target social networking and peer-to-peer (P2P) applications and websites. The use of these applications can lead to potential breaches in security on an organization's network. Security policies should include guidelines and restrictions for users of any social networking application or website.

Validation of Training Effectiveness

If an organization invests in security awareness and training, it should also make sure that the training is effective. Effective training helps to ensure compliance and increases the overall security of the organization.

To validate the effectiveness of your security awareness and training program, you'll need to identify which components of those programs will have the most impact on overall security.

The SANS Securing the Human Program offers some free tools to help organizations establish metrics for measuring impact or behavioral changes that can be attributed to the training along with metrics for tracking compliance and ways to assess various risks. For more information, you may visit

http://www.securingthehuman.org/resources/metrics

Integrate Systems and Data with Third Parties

Business Partners

A business partner is a commercial entity that has a relationship of some sort with another, separate commercial entity. A business partner can be a supplier, customer, agent, reseller or vendor of similar products or services. Business partnership can be formal, such as a contractual agreement or informal, but no matter what type of partnership exists, there will always be the need to share information among business partners.

In order to properly adhere to security protocols, business partners should go through an on-boarding and off-boarding process when the relationship both begins and concludes, respectively. Proper on-boarding involves acclimating partners to security practices that you expect them to follow. This ensures that there will be a fair balance of responsibility and liability in the partnership. Likewise, when the partnership ends, you should establish an off-boarding process. Both parties should agree to terminate any integration, including loss of cross-organizational access and other controls that are no longer necessary.

Social Media Networks and Applications

Social media networks and applications such as Facebook, Twitter, LinkedIn and Yammer are being incorporated into more business scenarios than ever before. Companies leverage the power of these platforms to connect with a more public-facing audience in order to expand their media presence. However, the public nature of social media and related apps often presents a risk to an organization's security. Employees may post sensitive information on a social network that has wider-reaching consequences than simple word-of-mouth. Even on its official web page, a company might reveal more than it should. The openness of social media is also a haven for social engineers who will attempt to deceive employees into compromising security.

Even within private social networks like Yammer, security professionals need to exercise caution. Are your administrators adequately trained on the particular service you're using? Are they given the proper tools to moderate the network? What are some of your privacy considerations as you try to keep sensitive information from leaking? Since you're relying on a third party to provide the service, there will always be a certain measure of control that you lack with social media.

Interoperability Agreements

There are various types of agreements that business entities may rely on to facilitate interoperability. Some of these agreements are:

Service-level agreement (SLA)

The agreement clearly defines what services are to be provided to the client and what support, if any, will be provided. Services may include everything from hardware and software to human resources. A strong SLA will outline basic service expectations for liability purposes.

Business partner agreement (BPA)

This agreement defines how a partnership between business entities will be conducted and what exactly is expected of each entity in terms of services, finances and security. For security purposes, BPAs should describe exactly what the partners are willing to share with each other and how any inter-organizational access will be handled.

Memorandum of understanding (MOU)

This type of agreement is usually not legally binding and typically does not involve the exchange money. MOUs are less formal than traditional contracts, but still have a certain degree of significance to all parties involved. They are typically enacted as a way to express a desire for all parties to achieve the same goal in the agreed-upon manner. They are intended to be mutually beneficial without involving courts of money. Because they typically have no legal foundation, MOUs are not the most secure agreement for a partnership.

Interconnection security agreement (ISA)

This type of agreement is geared toward the information systems of partnered entities to ensure that the use of inter-organizational technology meets a certain security standard. Because they focus heavily on security, ISAs are often written to be legally binding. ISAs can also support MOUs to increase their security viability.

Risk Awareness

In any sort of business arrangement or third-party integration, all parties should be aware of the inherent risks involved in the relationship. Risk awareness involves being consistently informed about the details of day-to-day interoperability. Likewise, all employees should be trained in spotting risk in their own departments, no matter how large or small. When employees evaluate the role they play in a partnership or social media integration, they will get a better idea of the risks that they are susceptible to. Delegating this responsibility will foster a culture of risk awareness and prepare an organization for risk management.

Data Sharing and Backups

In business partnerships and other third-party relationships, data sharing is often integral to the cooperative process. Allowing a trusted party access to your data will hopefully strengthen the support that they give you in whatever capacity you deem fit. However, even those you trust in a business arrangement should not necessarily be given total access to the data your organization independently owns. Although you may be able to implement some form of access control to limit what is shared, the human element can render these controls ineffective. You should clearly define what you consider unauthorized sharing based on what data must remain strictly confidential and caution your employees to abide by these regulations. Any policies that discuss data ownership and sharing with third parties may also include legal ramifications for employees who engage in unauthorized sharing.

A similar concern is how you should handle data backups. You may not want to allow your partners to back up all data that you've shared with them. Some sensitive data is considered volatile and should not be kept in any sort of permanent storage capacity. Data that you share and that a partner backs up may fall into the wrong hands, out of your control.

Guidelines for Securely Integrating Systems and Data with Third Parties

Follow these guidelines for securely integrating systems and data with third parties:

- Consider developing and following procedures for on-boarding and off-boarding business partners as the organizational dynamics change.
- Draft the appropriate interoperability agreement for your security needs when working with partners.
- Follow all security policies and procedures defined in the agreement.
- Review agreement requirements to verify compliance and performance standards.
- Exercise discretion in using social media networks when publishing business information to a wide audience.
- Ensure that employees follow best security practices when using social media.
- Encourage risk awareness in all levels of your organization.
- Clearly define data ownership from the onset of a business arrangement.
- Tightly control data sharing and caution employees not to engage in unauthorized sharing of data.
- Set rules for backing up volatile data so that it does not fall out of your control.

Chapter 8 - Risk

Management

Risk Analysis

How do you know what to protect your organization against? What constitutes a risk? You need to find out what exactly will help you determine what a risk is on your system or network.

Risk Management

If a risk is not managed correctly, it could result in disclosure, modification, loss, destruction or interruption of a critical asset. Risk management is a cyclical process that includes four phases:

- Identify and assess risks that exist in a system.
- Analyze the potential impact risks will have on a system.
- Formulate a strategy on how to respond to risks.
- Mitigate the impact of risks for future security.

Security Assessment Types

Assessing an organization's security infrastructure will determine whether current security measures are acceptable. The three general categories of assessment are:

1. Risk

   A risk assessment is an evaluation of an organization, a portion of an organization, an information system or system components to assess the security risk. Risk assessments are usually performed as part of the risk analysis process to identify what parts or functions of the business pose the highest risk.

2. Threat

   A threat assessment is an evaluation of known threats to an organization and the potential damage to business operations and systems. Threat assessment is usually performed as part of the risk analysis process, but could be performed at any time to verify the current security controls are still operating successfully and are detecting and managing threats. An important element in this assessment is determining the path or means by which an attacker can carry out a security attack or threat vector.

3. Vulnerability

   A vulnerability assessment is an evaluation used to find security weaknesses within an organization. Vulnerability assessments can be performed on an organization's physical security implementations and all networks, hardware and software.

Types of Risk

Security risks are often identified as natural, man-made or system risks, depending on their source.

Natural

Natural risks are related to weather or other uncontrollable events that are residual occurrences of the activities of nature. Different types of natural disasters include earthquakes, wildfires, flooding, blizzards, tsunamis, hurricane, tornadoes and landslides.

Man-made

Man-made risks are residual occurrences of individual or collective human activity. Man-made events can be caused intentionally or unintentionally.

Intentional man-made attacks include arson, terrorist attacks, political unrest, break-ins, theft of equipment and/or data, equipment damage, file destruction and information disclosure.

Unintentional man-made risks include user computing mistakes, social networking and cloud computing, Excessive employee illnesses or epidemics and Information disclosure.

System

System risks are related to any weakness or vulnerability found within a network, service, application or device. System risks include unsecured mobile devices, unstable virtualization environments, unsecured network devices, email vulnerabilities, such as viruses and spam and account management vulnerabilities, such as unassigned privileges.

Components of Risk Analysis

Risk is the likelihood that a threat can exploit a vulnerability to cause some type of damage. The severity of the risk is based on how much damage the risk could cause and how likely it is to occur.

Vulnerability-Assessed Threats

Examples of vulnerability-assessed threats include:

- If a business is located next to railroad tracks and a train derails, leaking toxic fluids, the business might be forced into inactivity for a number of days.
- If key manufacturing staff express their plans to strike, they may threaten to damage equipment beforehand to heighten the impact of their impending actions.
- A key supplier may be unable to provide raw materials for the production of an organization's principal products.

Phases of Risk Analysis

When determining how to protect computer networks, computer installations and information, risk analysis is the security process used for assessing risk damages that can affect an organization.

There are six phases in the risk analysis process:

1. Asset Identification
   Identifying the assets that require protection and determining the value of the assets.

2. Vulnerability identification
   Identifying vulnerabilities so that the analyst can confirm where asset protection problems exist. Locating weaknesses exposes the critical areas that are most susceptible to vulnerabilities. Vulnerability scanning is a method used to determine weaknesses in systems. This method can, however, produce false positives which tend

to initiate reasons for concern, even when there are no actual issues or weaknesses in the system.

3. Threat assessment
   Once vulnerabilities are understood, the threats that may take advantage of or exploit those vulnerabilities are determined.

4. Probability quantification
   Quantifying the likelihood or probability that threats will exploit vulnerabilities.

5. Impact analysis
   Once the probabilities are determined, the impact of these potential threats need to be evaluated. This can include either the impact of recovering from the damage or the impact of implementing possible preventive measures.

6. Countermeasures determination
   Determining and developing countermeasures to eliminate or reduce risks. The countermeasures must be economically sound and provide the expected level of protection. In other words, the countermeasures must not cost more than the expected loss caused by threats that exploit vulnerabilities.

Risk Analysis Methods

Qualitative

Qualitative analysis methods use descriptions and words to measure the amount and impact of risk. E.g., ratings can be high, medium or low based on the criteria used to analyze the impact. Qualitative analysis is generally scenario based. A weakness of qualitative risk analysis lies with its sometimes subjective and untestable methodology.

Quantitative

Quantitative analysis is based completely on numeric values. Data is analyzed using historic records, experiences, industry best practices and records, statistical theories, testing and experiments. This methodology may be weak in situations where risk is not easily quantifiable.

Semi-quantitative

The semi-quantitative analysis method uses a description that is associated with a numeric value. It is neither fully qualitative nor quantitative. This methodology attempts to find a middle ground between the previous two risk analysis types.

Risk Calculation

Risk calculation focuses on financial and operational loss impact and locates threat exploitation indicators in an organization. Risk calculation can be viewed as a formula that takes into account the worth of each asset, the potential impact of each risk and the likelihood of each threat and then weighs that against the potential costs of alleviating system vulnerabilities. Organizations may use this process to determine single loss expectancy (SLE) or the annual loss expectancy (ALE) for each risk identified. The SLE value represents the financial loss that is expected from a specific adverse event. The Ale value is calculated by multiplying an SLE by its annual rate of occurrence (ARO) to determine the total cost of a risk to an organization on an annual basis.

Calculating Risk

A company might calculate that a certain system in its demilitarized zone (DMZ) has almost 90 percent probability of experiencing a port scan attack on a daily basis. However, although the threat level is high, the company does not consider the system to be at much risk of damage from the threat of a scan. The cost of hardening the system to completely prevent the scan far outweighs the potential losses due to the identified risk.

On the other hand, a company might determine that its server room is at a high risk of complete loss due to a natural disaster and that the cost of such a loss would be catastrophic for the organization. Although the likelihood of the disaster threat is quite low, the overall impact is so great that the company maintains an expensive alternate site that it can switch operations to in the event of such an emergency.

Vulnerability Tables

A simple vulnerability table is often a strategic tool for completing a vulnerability assessment. The following table lists details associated with various vulnerabilities.

Vulnerability	Identification Source	Risk of Occurrence (1=Low; 5=High)	Impact Estimate (US Dollars)	Mitigation
Flood damage	Physical plant	5	$95,000	Physical adjustments and flood insurance
Electrical failure	Physical plant	2	$100,000	Generator, Uninterruptible Power Supply (UPs)
Flu epidemic	Personnel	4	$200,000	Flu shots

Using a table allows planners to identify the likelihood of threats or vulnerabilities, record the possible impact and then prioritize mitigation efforts. Mitigation helps reduce the impact of an exploited vulnerability. A loss of power has a relatively high risk with a reasonable mitigation effort, consisting of a one-time expenditure to purchase a backup generator.

If there were two additional columns in the table, the assessment would be more useful, as in the following example.

Vulnerability	Cost of Mitigation	Vulnerability Impact Post Mitigation
Electrical failure	$500 for generator	$0

Risk Response Strategies

Once risk is identified, you may examine a response strategy to determine the appropriate action to take. Multiple strategies may even be combined into a single response. There are five common strategies used as described below.

Avoidance

This is used to eliminate the risk altogether by eliminating the cause. This may be as simple as putting an end to the operation or entity that is at risk, like shutting down a server that is a frequent target of attack.

Transference

This is used to allocate the responsibility of risk to another agency, or to a third party, such as an insurance company.

Acceptance

This is the acknowledgement and acceptance of the risk and consequences that come with it, if that risk were to materialize. Acceptance does not mean leaving a system completely vulnerable, but recognizing that the risk involved is not entirely avoidable.

Mitigation

These techniques protect against possible attacks and are implemented when the impact of a potential risk is substantial.

Mitigation may come in the form of active defenses like intrusion detection systems (IDs), or cautionary measures like backing up at-risk data.

Deterrence

This involves applying changes to the conditions to make it less likely or enticing for an attacker to launch an attack. Deterrent factors may include physical security like checkpoints inside and outside of a building. A virtual intruder might be deterred in knowing that a strong system defense may be able to track and identify them to the authorities.

Risk Mitigation and Control Types

Risk can be mitigated by implementing the appropriate security controls. The major control types are explained below.

Technical Controls

Hardware of software installations that are implemented to monitor and prevent threats and attacks to computer systems and services. For example, installing and configuring a network firewall is a type of technical control.

Management Controls

Procedures implemented to monitor the adherence to organizational security policies. These controls are specifically designed to control the operational efficiencies of a particular area and to monitor security policy compliance. For example, annual or regularly scheduled security scans and audits to check for compliance with security policies.

Operational controls

Security measures implemented to safeguard all aspects of day-to-day operations, functions and activities. For example, door locks and guards at entrances are controls used to permit only authorized personnel into a building.

Loss Controls

Also called damage controls, these are security measures implemented to protect key assets from being damaged. This includes reducing the chances of a loss occurring and reducing the severity of a loss when one occurs. For example, fire extinguishers and sprinkler systems can reduce property damage in the event of a fire.

Implement Vulnerability Assessment Tools and Techniques

Vulnerability Assessment Techniques

Assessing the current state of security implementations for an organization is crucial to ensuring all threats and vulnerabilities have been addressed. Below are common techniques that can be used to carry out security assessments.

Review the baseline report

A baseline report is a collection of security and configuration settings that are to be applied to a particular system or network in the organization. The baseline report is a benchmark against which you can compare other systems in your network. When creating a baseline for a particular computer, the settings you decide to include will depend on its operating system and its function in your organization and should include manufacturer recommendations.

Perform code reviews

Regular code reviews should be conducted for all applications in development. Reviews may be carried out manually by a developer or automatically using a source code analysis tool. Both methods are useful in identifying potential weaknesses in an application that may eventually lead to an attack if not corrected.

Determine attack surface

The attack surface is the combination of all points in a system or application that are exposed and available to attackers. By reducing the points in an attack surface, you will be less vulnerable to possible attacks.

Review the security architecture

A security architecture review is an evaluation of an organization's current security infrastructure model and measures. Regular reviews are important to determine if current systems and critical assets are secured properly and if potential threats and vulnerabilities have been addressed. During this review, areas of concern are targeted and further evaluated to make sure security measures meet the current needs.

Review the security design

Security design reviews are completed before a security implementation is applied. Using the architectural review results, the reviewer can determine if the security solution will in fact fulfill the needs of an organization.

Vulnerability Assessment Tools

When assessing security for your system or systems, there are many software tools that are available. Tools can be found to scan for and detect a very wide range of vulnerabilities and specific hard-to-detect vulnerabilities. By running these tools, you can see exactly what potential attackers would see if they assessed your systems. However, their usefulness to you is dependent on how well you can interpret the results of security assessment tools. When you become acquainted with what to expect and what to look out for in a tool's results, you'll find it easier to remove any vulnerabilities in your system.

Below are different types of tools available for assessing your systems.

Protocol analyzer

Implement to assess traffic on a network and what it reveals about the protocols being used.

Sniffer (packet analyzer)

Implement to capture and assess individual data packets sent over a network.

Vulnerability scanner

Implement this application to assess your systems, networks and applications for weaknesses.

Port scanner

Implement to assess the current state of all ports on your network and to detect potential open ports that may pose risks to your organization.

Honeypot

Implement this environment to redirect suspicious activity away from legitimate network systems and onto an isolated system where you can monitor it safely.

Honeypots

A honeypot is a security tool that lures attackers away from legitimate network resources while tracking their activities. Honeypots appear and act as legitimate components of the network but are actually secure lockboxes where security professionals can block the intrusion and begin logging activity for use in court or even launch a counterattack. The act of luring individuals in could potentially be perceived as entrapment or violate the code of ethics of your organization. These legal and ethical issues should be discussed with your organization's legal counsel and human resources department.

Honeypots can be software emulation programs, hardware decoys or an entire dummy network, known as a honeynet. A honeypot implementation often includes some kind of IDS to facilitate monitoring and tracking of intruders. Some dedicated honeypot software packages can be specialized types of IDSs.

Scan for Vulnerabilities

The Hacking Process

Understanding the general steps of the hacking process will help you recognize attacks in progress and stop them before they cause damage.

Footprinting

Also known as profiling, in this step, the attacker chooses a target and begins to gather information that is publicly or readily available. With basic tools, such as a web browser and an Internet connection, an attacker can often determine the IP addresses of a company's Domain Name System (DNS) servers; the range of addresses assigned to the company; names, email addresses and phone numbers of contacts within the company; and the company's physical address. Attackers use dumpster diving or searching through garbage, to find sensitive information in paper form. The names and titles of people within the organization enable the attacker to begin social engineering to gain even more private information. The Hypertext Markup Language (HTML) code of a company's web page can provide information, such as IP addresses and names of web servers, operating system versions, file paths and names of developers or administrators. DNS servers are common footprinting targets because, if not properly secured, they can provide a detailed map of an organization's entire network infrastructure.

Scanning

Also called banner grabbing, the second step is to scan an organization's infrastructure or systems to see where vulnerabilities might lie. In this step, the attacker may use a network mapping tool such as Nmap or perform a ping sweep to determine which host IP addresses in the company's IP address range are active. The attacker will scan the target's border routers, firewalls, web servers and other systems that are directly connected to the Internet to see which services are listening on which ports and to determine the operating systems and manufacturers of each system. Additionally, the attacker might begin a war dialing campaign to determine if there are any vulnerabilities in the organization's telecommunications system. The attacker might even try war driving, which involves driving up to the company with a laptop and a wireless card to see if there are any wireless access points (APs) to provide a way into the network.

Enumerating

During this step, the attacker will try to gain access to resources or other information, such as users, groups and shares. The attacker can obtain this information through social engineering, network sniffing, dumpster diving, watching a user log in or searching for credentials written down at user workstations. If the attacker can obtain a valid user name, he can begin the process of cracking the user's password.

Attacking

Attacking is the last phase of the hack, in which the hacker attempts to cause damage or a service disruption or to steal or destroy sensitive information using various hacking tools.

Network Mappers

Network mapping tools are used to explore and gather network layout information from a network. A network map can be used to illustrate the physical connectivity of networks within an organization and can provide detailed information on hardware, services and traffic paths.

Ethical Hacking

In ethical hacking, a planned and approved attempt is made to penetrate the security defenses of a system in order to identify vulnerabilities. In an ethical hack, a friendly or designated hacker (a white hat) assumes the mindset of an attacker and attempts to breach security using any and all tools and techniques an attacker might employ. It may be performed by an employee on the company's behalf or by an outside firm contracted by the company.

Vulnerability Scanning and Penetration Testing

A vulnerability scan uses passive tools and security utilities to identify and quantify vulnerabilities within a system, such as lacking security controls and common misconfigurations, but does not directly test the security features of that system. Vulnerability scans may be credentialed, in that they implement credentials in order to ascertain vulnerabilities at the highest privilege levels or they may be non-credentialed, meaning they run without credentials to see what a hacker would see at a lower level. Like other scanning mechanisms, vulnerability scanners run the risk of producing false positives and false negatives.

A true penetration test or pen test, uses active tools and security utilities to evaluate security by simulating an attack on a system. A penetration test will verify that a threat exists, then will actively test and bypass security controls and will finally exploit vulnerabilities on the system. Penetration testing is less common and more intrusive than vulnerability scanning. While the information gained from a penetration test is often more thorough, there is a risk that the system may suffer actual damage because of the security breach.

Types of Vulnerability Scans

A vulnerability scan is one of the first steps in either an attack or an ethical hack. There are two main types of vulnerability scans for general vulnerabilities, such as scans for open ports; and application-specific scans, such as password crack against a particular operating system. You will use different scanning tools depending upon the type of scan you wish to run.

Box Testing Methods

When conducting a penetration test, the organization must examine the different testing methods and determine what information the tester will be given beforehand. Three main penetration test types are explained below.

Black box test

This refers to a situation where the tester is given no specific information about the structure of the system being tested. The tester may know what a system does, but know how it does it. This type of test would fall into the footprinting or scanning phase of the hacking process.

Grey box test

This refers to a situation where the tester has partial knowledge of internal architectures and systems or other preliminary information about the system being tested. This type of test would fall into the enumerating phase of the hacking process.

White box test

This refers to a situation when the tester knows about all aspects of the system and understands the function and design of the system before the test is conducted. This type of test is sometimes conducted as a follow-up to a black box test to fully evaluate flaws discovered during the black box test. This type of test would fall into the attacking phase of the hacking process.

Security Utilities

Any security or network tool can be used for ethical or unethical purposes. To perform an ethical hack, you will need to use the same tools employed by attackers. Some tools are generally available by downloading them from the Internet and some must be purchased from vendors. Because tools and utilities are constantly changing, it is important to continually research the available tools and their functions.

There are many different tools available for different security tasks and some have multiple uses.

Vulnerability scanning

Microsoft Baseline Security Analyzer (MBSA), Nessus®, SAINT, Nmap Security Scanner, GFI LANguard™, OpenVAS

Port scanning

Nmap Security Scanner, Snort, Netcat, SuperScan, ShieldsUP, hping

Password scanning and cracking

John the Ripper, Cain & Abel, THC Hydra, Pwdump, Ophcrack, Medusa

Exploits, Trojan horses and "stress testers"

Metasploit, Social Engineer toolkit, w3af, Core Impact, sqlmap

Intrusion detection

Snort, NFR® BackOfficer Friendly, IDScenter, Fport, OSSIM

Network and security administration

Webmin, Tripwire®, Bastille, PuTTY, HiSecWeb

Protocol analyzer or packet sniffer

Wireshark, NetStumbler, dsniff, OmniPeek, Ettercap, Microsoft Message Analyzer, tcpdump, WinDump, Cain & Abel

Mitigation and Deterrent Techniques

The IT security team should plan for worst-case scenarios and should have strong mitigation and deterrent techniques in place, should something go wrong.

Security Posture

Security posture is the position an organization takes on securing all aspects of its business. Strong security posture includes an initial baseline configuration for all organization, continuous security monitoring methods and remediation techniques, as well as strict mitigation and deterrent methods.

DLP

Data loss/leak prevention (DLP) is a software solution that detects and prevents sensitive information in a system from being stolen or otherwise falling into the wrong hands. The software actively monitors data in any state – whether in use or at rest – and detects any unauthorized attempts to destroy, move or copy that data. If any suspicious activity is detected, some DLP software is able to block users from interacting with data in specific ways.

For example, a security administrator might put a DLP system in place on the corporate network to detect any attempt to send confidential files over email and then prevent that email from reaching its destination. In this respect, data loss prevention has the opposite goal of an intrusion detection/prevention system; instead of focusing on inbound attacks, DLP software protects outbound data. The malicious transfer of data from one system to another is called data exfiltration.

Data Loss vs. Leakage

Although related, data loss and data leakage are not entirely the same. Data that is leaked is transferred to unauthorized parties, but may still exist in its original form and location. Data that is lost is transferred to unauthorized parties and is no longer in its owners' possession.

Detection Controls and Prevention Controls

Detection controls are implemented to monitor a situation or activity and react to any irregular activities by bringing the issue to the attention of administrators. Prevention controls are similar to detection controls, but instead of just monitoring for irregularities, they can react by blocking access completely – thereby preventing damage to a system, building or network.

The decision to detect or prevent attacks or unacceptable traffic is based on risk. If there is a high risk of damage to the network or organization due to a Denial of Service (DoS) attack, a prevention control that blocks the attack is most appropriate. Detection controls are best employed when experience shows that little or no threat to network security exists and a warning of possible problems is sufficient. For example, a surveillance camera will monito and detect when access is attempted, but it cannot prevent access. However, if a guard is placed at the access point, then he or she could not only detect, but also prevent access if it is unauthorized.

Blocking Techniques

Blocking techniques include logging the user off a system or reconfiguring the firewall to block the source.

Risk Mitigation Strategies

Risk mitigation techniques can be applied at many levels of an organization to help guard against potential risk damage. Below are some of the most effect techniques for mitigating risk.

Policies and procedures

Policies and procedures can be implemented so an organization can enforce conduct rules among employees. It is crucial for an organization to distribute the appropriate policies in order to reduce the likelihood of damage to assets and to prevent data loss or theft. Policies and procedures can include:

- Privacy policy
- Acceptable use policy (AUP)
- Security policy
- Mandatory vacation procedures
- Job rotation procedures
- Audit policy
- Password policy

- Separation of duties guidelines
- Least privilege guidelines

Auditing and reviews

Perform routine audits to assess the risk of a particular operation and to verify that the current security controls in place are operating properly to secure the organization. Be sure to review existing user rights and permissions to make sure they meet your needs for confidentiality as well as accessibility of information and resources.

Security controls

Proper implementation of the appropriate technical, management and operational controls is a powerful way to mitigate both general and specific risks.

Change management

Good change management practices can mitigate unintentional internal risks caused by inappropriate alterations to systems, tools or the environment.

Incident management

Organizations must deal with security incidents as they arise and good management strategies can mitigate the severity of damage caused by risks.

Types of Mitigation and Deterrent Techniques

Common techniques for monitoring vulnerabilities and mitigating issues as soon as they are detected are described below.

Performance and system monitoring

Performance and system monitoring enable you to monitor and diagnose the system and network for potential problems. In Windows® systems, performance monitoring is available on the Administrative Tools menu. This tool can be used to quickly monitor some elements of the operation of your system. You can also gather real-time data, export data to be used in a separate program, send administrative alerts based on predefined criteria, create a performance baseline, detect network issues and manage server performance.

Monitoring system logs

Reviewing the activity recorded in log files can reveal a great deal about a suspected attack, Log files that should be monitored regularly on a set schedule are:

- Event logs
- Audit logs
- Security logs
- Access logs

Manual bypassing of electronic controls

Electronic controls are common in securing an organization's building, server rooms and other highly secure areas. When the electronic controls have been tampered with and there is a security breach by any unauthorized individual, a manual bypass control should be implemented. This gives authorized personnel the ability to bypass the electronic control and ensure that the area is locked down and remains secure.

Hardening

General hardening procedures should be considered as a mitigation technique. In particular, the following security measures should be enforced to provide a higher level of security:

- Disable all unnecessary services
- Ensure that the management interface and applications are properly protected.
- Password protect all accounts.
- Disable all unnecessary accounts.
- Establish appropriate detection and prevention controls based on the needs of the organization.

Applying port security

Properly securing the ports on your network will prevent attackers from carrying out port scanning activities to gain information about your network. Security measures include:

- Configuring port authentication (802.1x)
- Disabling all unused ports

Reporting

Regular system reporting procedures should be in place to manage and enhance system capabilities. There are three reporting methods that can be utilized to support mitigation efforts made within a system:

- Alarms are used to bring attention to a fault condition in the system.
- Alerts are used to communicate that a condition has occurred and needs attention before it shuts down.

- Trends are a snapshot of the system performance across a specified time frame.

Implementing physical security

Applying proper physical security controls and measures can be an effective deterrent technique to discourage attackers from attempting to gain access to the building, grounds, systems, resources and data. Examples might include fencing, door locks, surveillance cameras and systems and guards.

Failsafe, Failsecure and Failopen

Failsafe, Failsecure and Failopen are different ways that systems can be designed to perform when those systems cease to operate or when certain conditions are met. For example, most push lawn mowers are designed with some sort of lever that must be held in position by an operator in order for the blades to function. If that lever is released, the blades stop. This type of failsafe design is implemented to prevent harm to individuals.

A common application of this design consideration is in an organization's physical access control systems. In the event of a power failure, electric door strikes cannot be operated, so they are failsecure devices because they keep doors secured without power. Mechanical crashbars are failsafe devices in that they can be added to the inside of those doors to permit people to safely exit, even though the electric strike has no power. A magnetic lock is an example of a failopen device, as it leaves the door unsecured in the event of a power failure. For example, a school's exterior doors may be designed to failopen so that the fire alarm system could cut power to them to permit students and faculty to exit and emergency responders to get in, whereas the server room might be designed as failsafe/failsecure to permit staff to exit while still keeping unauthorized people out.

Chapter 9 –

Troubleshooting and

Managing Security

Incidents

Respond to Security Incidents

Security Incident Management

A security incident is a specific instance of a risk event occurring, whether or not it causes damage. Security incident management is the set of practices and procedures that govern how an organization will respond to an incident in progress that govern how an organization will respond to an incident in progress. The goals of incident management are to contain the incident appropriately and ultimately minimize any damage that may occur as a result of the incident. Incident management typically includes procedures to log and report on all identified incidents and the actions taken in response.

An organization may create a task force to manage all aspects of incident management within the organization.

Computer Crimes

A computer crime is a criminal act that involves using a computer as a source or target, instead of an individual. It can involve stealing restricted information by hacking into a system, compromising national security, perpetrating fraud, conducting illegal activity or spreading malicious code. It may be committed via the Internet or a private network.

IRPs

An Incident Response Policy (IRP) is the security policy that determines the actions that an organization will take following a confirmed or potential security breach. The IRP usually specifies:

- Preparation measures like researching known and likely threats.

- Who determines and declares if an actual security incident has occurred.

- How they go about this incident identification.

- What individuals or departments will receive notifications?

- How and when they are notified.

- Who will respond to the incident?

- Guidelines for the appropriate response, including mitigation steps to take.

- When the response needs escalation to more qualified personnel.

First Responders

A first responder is the first experienced person or team of trained professionals that arrive on an incident scene. In a non-IT environment, this term can be used to define the first trained person – such as a police officer or firefighter – to respond to an accident, damage site or natural disaster. In the IT world, first responders can include security professionals, human resource personnel or IT support professionals.

Chain of Custody

The chain of custody is the record of evidence handling from collection through presentation in court. The evidence can be hardware components, electronic data or telephone systems. The chain of evidence reinforces the integrity and proper custody of evidence from collection, to analysis, to storage and finally to presentation. Every person in the chain who handles evidence must log the methods and tools they used.

Incident Isolation

When computer crimes are reported, one of the first response activities is quarantining affected devices to separate them from the rest of the devices in a system. Separation can be both physical and virtual. Doing this prevents the affected devices from altering other elements of a system or vice versa. Devices can also be completely removed from the crime location. They are tagged with a chain of custody record to begin the process of making the evidence secure for future presentation in court.

Computer Forensics

Computer forensics is the skill that deals with collecting and analyzing data from storage devices, computer systems, networks and wireless communications and presenting this information as a form of evidence in a court of law. Primarily, forensics deals with the recovery and investigation of potential evidence.

Order of Volatility

Data is volatile and the ability to retrieve or validate data after a security incident depends on where it is stored in a location or memory layer of a computer or external device. E.g., data on backup and thumb drives can last for years while data in random-access memory (RAM) may last only for nanoseconds.

The order in which you need to recover data after an incident before the data deteriorates, is erased, or is overwritten is known as the order of volatility. The general order of volatility for storage devices is:

- Registers, cache and RAM.

- Network caches and virtual memory.

- Hard drives and flash drives.

- CD-ROMs, DVD-ROMs and printouts.

Basic Forensic Process

There are four basic phases in a forensic process:

Collection phase

- Identify the attacked system and label it.

- Record and acquire details from all related personnel who have access to the system, as well as the evidence material, keeping in mind the integrity of the data.

Examination phase

- Use automated and manual methods to forensically process collected data.

- Assess and extract the evidence, keeping in mind the integrity of the data.

Analysis phase

- Analyze the results of the examination phase using methods and techniques permissible by law.

- Obtain useful information that justifies the reason for the collection and examination.

Reporting phase

- Report the results of the forensic analysis, including a description of the tools and methods used and why things were done that way.

- Brainstorm different ways to improve existing security controls and provide recommendations for better policies, tools, procedures and other methods in a forensic process.

Basic Forensic Response Procedures for IT

Forensic response procedures for IT help security professionals collect evidence from data in a form that is admissible in a court of law.

Capture system image

Capturing exact duplicates of the evidence, also known as forensic images is accomplished by making a bit-for-bit copy of a piece of media as an image file with high accuracy.

Examine network traffic and logs

Logs record everything that happens in an intrusion prevention system (IPS) or intrusion detection system (IDS) and in routers, firewalls, servers, desktops, mainframes, applications, databases, antivirus software and virtual private networks (VPNs). With these logs, it is possible to extract the identity of hackers and provide the evidence needed.

Capture video

Video forensics is the method by which video is scrutinized for clues. Tools for computer forensics are used in reassembling video to be used as evidence in a court of law.

Record time offset

The format in which time is recorded against a file activity, such as file creation, deletion, last modified and last accessed, has developed to incorporate a local time zone offset against GMT. This makes it easier for forensics to determine the exact time the activity took place even if the computer is moved from one time zone to another or if the time zone has deliberately been changed on a system.

Take hashes

Federal law enforcement agencies and federal governments maintain a list of files such as files relating to components of Microsoft® Windows® and other application software. The hash codes generated by a file or software can be compared to the list of known file hashes and hacker tools if any are flagged or marked as unknown.

Take screenshots

You should capture screenshots of each and every step of a forensic procedure, especially when you are retrieving evidence using a forensic tool. This will ensure that data present on a compromised system is not tampered with and also provides the court with proof of your use of valid computer forensic methods while extracting the evidence.

Identify witnesses

Courts generally accept evidence if it is seconded by the testimony of a witness who observed the procedure by which the evidence was acquired. A computer forensics expert witness is someone who has experience in handling computer forensic tools and is able to establish the validity of evidence.

Track man hours and expense

When the first incidents of computer crimes occurred, it would take less than 40 hours to complete a forensic investigation because incidents involved single computers. Now, with advances in technology and the advent of new digital media such as voice recorders, cameras, laptop computers and mobile devices, computer forensics procedures can take an exponentially greater amount of man hours and expenses. Also, the increase in storage device capacities and encryption affect the amount of man hors that it can take to assess any damage and consequently increase expenses incurred in any computer forensics investigation. Capturing this expense is part of the overall damage assessment for the incident.

Big Data Analysis

Accurately securing, collecting and evaluating big data sets is especially difficult because big data implementations often lack a consistent structure and have a variety of different sources. There are general characteristics that you should look for when responding to a data breach, which also apply to big data:

- Unformatted or incorrectly formatted data.
- Incomplete or missing data.
- Invalid data.
- Data that is out of range.
- Data that is duplicated.

Guidelines for Responding to Security Incidents

Once an incident has been identified, the response team or security administrator must investigate all aspects of the security crime.

- If an IRP exists, then follow the guidelines outlined to respond to the incident.
- If an IRP does not exist, then determine a primary investigator who will lead the team through the investigation process.
- Determine if the events actually occurred and to what extent a system or process was damaged.
- Document the incident.

- Assess the damage and determine the impact on affected systems.
- Determine if outside expertise is needed, such as a consultant firm.
- Notify local law enforcement, if needed.
- Secure the scene, so that the hardware is contained.
- Collect all the necessary evidence, which may be electronic data, hardware components or telephony system components. Observe the order of volatility as you gather electronic data from various media.
- Interview personnel to collect additional information pertaining to the crime.
- Report the investigation's findings to the required people.

Recover from a Security Incident

To fully recover from the incident, you must not only know how to fix the network, but also how to describe the problem to the key decision makers at your company so that future incidents can be avoided.

Basic Incident Recovery Process

The basic process for incident recovery is relatively simple:

1. Asses the level of damage caused by the incident.
2. Recover from the incident.
3. Report the incident.

Damage Assessment

During or after a security incident, a damage assessment should be done to determine the extent of damage, the origin or cause of the incident and the amount of expected downtime. The assessment can also determine the appropriate strategy to employ as you move into the recovery phase.

Recovery Methods

After assessing the damage, you will know the extent of recovery that needs to be done. Many organizations rely on reformatting the system in the case of a rootkit code attack, applying software patches or reloading system software in the case of a virus or malicious code infestation and restoring backups in the case of an intrusion or backdoor attack. Recovery methods can also involve replacing hardware in the case of a physical security incident.

Incident Reports

An incident report is a report that includes a description of the events that occurred during a security incident. Care should be taken to write as much detail relating to an incident as possible, such as the name of the organization, the nature of the event, names and phone numbers of contacts, the time and date of an event and log information. However, a report should not be delayed because of problems with gathering information. Further probes can be carried out after the report has been written.

Guidelines for Recovering from a Security Incident

Damage assessment, recovery and reporting are important in dealing with an incident.

Steps while assessing the damage in a security incident

- Assess the area of damage to determine the next course of action.
- Determine the amount of damage to the facility, hardware, systems and networks.
- If your company has suffered digital – rather than physical – damage, you may need to examine log files, identify which

accounts have been compromised and identify which files have been modified during the attack.

- If your company has suffered physical – and not digital – damage, you may need to take a physical inventory to determine which devices have been stolen or damaged, which areas he intruder(s) had access to and how many devices may have been damaged or stolen.
- One of the most important and overlooked components of damage assessment is to determine if the attack is over; attempting to react to an attack that is still in progress could do more harm than good.

Steps you may take when recovering from a security incident

- Replace hardware and network cables in case any have been damaged or stolen.
- Detect and delete malware and viruses from the affected systems and media.
- Disconnect the intruded systems from the servers and shut down the server to avoid further intrusions.
- Disable access to user accounts that have affected the network and search for all the backdoor software installed by the intruder.
- Establish that your organization is no longer exposed to a threat by scanning the networks and systems using an IDS.
- Reconnect the servers to the network.
- Restore the data and network systems from the most recent backup.
- Replace compromised data and applications or reformat the system and perform a fresh installation of the operating system.
- Harden the networks and servers by changing passwords, installing patches and reconfiguring firewalls and routers.
- Inform company officials and important stakeholders of the incident and if an insider was the source of the incident, reprimand the individual responsible according to company

policies or contact law enforcement to take action depending on the extent of the attack.

- Write a report describing the recovery process. A summary of the report should be saved for use in future security incident responses.

Details to capture when reporting a security incident

- The name of the organization.
- The name and phone number of the person who discovered the incident.
- The name(s) and phone number(s) of first responder(s).
- The type of event; for instance, a physical attack, malicious code attack or network attack.
- The date and time of the event, including the time zone.
- The source and destination of systems and networks, including IP addresses.
- The operating system and antivirus software used and their versions.
- The methods used to detect the incident; for instance, logs or IDSs.
- The business impact of the incident.
- The resolution steps taken.

Chapter 10 - Business Continuity and Disaster Recovery Planning

Business Continuity

BCPs

A business continuity plan (BCP) is a policy that defines how an organization will maintain normal day-to-day business operations in the event of business disruption or crisis. The BCP should be reviewed and tested on a regular basis. The plan must have executive support to be considered authoritative; the authorizing executive should personally sign the plan.

BIA

A business impact analysis (BIA) is a preparation step in BCP development that identifies present organizational risks and determines the impact to ongoing, business-critical operations and processes if such risks actually occur. BIAs contain vulnerability assessments and evaluations to determine risks and their impact.

MTD

Maximum tolerable downtime (MTD) is the longest period of time that a business outage may occur without causing irrecoverable business failure. The MTS limits the amount of recovery time that a business has to resume operations.

RPO

The recovery point objective (RPO) is the point in time, relative to a disaster, where the data recovery process begins. In IT systems it is often the point in time when the last successful backup is performed before a disruptive event occurs.

RTO

The recovery time objective (RTO) is the length of time within which normal business operations and activities can be restored following a disturbance. It includes the necessary recovery time to return the RPO and reinstate the system and resume processing from its current status. The RTO must be achieved before the MTD. Mean time to recovery (MTTR) is the average time taken for a business to recover from an incident or failure and is an offset of the RTO. If MTTR exceeds the given RTO, then business operations need to switch to the alternate site.

Continuity of Operations Plan

A continuity of operations plan is the component of the BCP that provides best practices to mitigate risks and best measures to recover from the impact of an incident. An effective continuity of operations plan can include:

Auditing of resources, staff and operational management

- Auditing storage facilities, data centers, operating systems and software and applications.

- Auditing networks such as the LAN and WAN, including remote access and authentication systems.

- Analyzing comprehensive risk and vulnerability.

- Creating data backups, recovery methods and emergency response procedures.

- Establishing a process on how to manage operations during a disaster.

Alternate Sites

As part of a BCP, an organization can maintain various types of alternate sites that can be used to restore system functions. A hot site is a fully configured alternate network that can be online quickly after a disaster. A warm site is a location that is dormant or performs non-critical functions under normal conditions, but which can be rapidly converted to a key operations site if needed. A cold site is a predetermined alternate location where a network can be rebuilt after a disaster.

IT Contingency Planning

An IT contingency plan is a component of the BCP that specifies alternate IT contingency procedures that you can switch over to when you are faced with an attack or disruption of service leading to a disaster for an organization. The effectiveness of an IT contingency plan depends upon:

- Key personnel understanding the components of the plan and when and how it should be initiated when the organization is facing an attack or disruption of service.

- Reviewing a checklist from time to time to see that all the aspects of an IT contingency plan are in place, such as recovery strategies including alternate sites.

- Providing adequate training to employees and management to exercise the contingency plan and maintaining the plan and reexamining it from time to time.

Succession Planning

A succession plan ensures that all key business personnel who can perform critical functions when needed, have one or more designated backups. A succession plan identifies the individuals, who they can replace, which functions they can perform and how they need to be trained.

Business Continuity Testing Methods

Paper Testing Methods

- Reviewing plan contents. Because they are familiar with the BCP construction, plan developers review the BCP's contents.
- Analyzing the solution. Senior management and division and department heads perform an additional analysis to ensure that the business continuity solution fulfills organizational recovery requirements.
- Using checklists. Checklists confirm whether the BCP meets predetermined, documented business needs.

Performing walkthroughs

Walkthroughs specifically focus on each BCP phase. Planners and testers walk through the individual steps to validate the logical flow of the sequence of events as a group.

This test is used to ensure that systems perform adequately at any alternate offsite facility, without taking the main site offline. Simulations effectively test the validity and compliance of the BCP.

Cutover

This test mimics an actual business disruption by shutting down the original site to test transfer and migration procedures to the alternate site and to test operations in the presence of an emergency.

Plan for Disaster Recovery

DRPs

A disaster recovery plan (DRP) is a plan that prepares an organization to react appropriately if the worst were to happen, be it a natural or a man-made disaster and provides the means to recover from such disaster without the loss of much time and money. A DRP can include:

- A list and contact information of individuals responsible for recovery.

- An inventory of hardware and software.

- A record of important business and customer information that you would require to continue business.

- A record of procedure manuals and other critical information such as the BCP and IT contingency plans.

- Specifications for alternate sites.

Fault Tolerance

Fault tolerance is the ability of a network or system to withstand a foreseeable component failure and continue to provide an acceptable level of service. There are several categories of fault tolerance measures, including those that protect power sources, disks and data storage and network components. Fault tolerant systems often employ some kind of duplication or redundancy of resources to maintain functionality if one component is damaged or fails.

Redundancy Measures

Mean time to failure (MTTF) is the rating that predicts the length of time that a device or component is expected to be operational. MTTF is generally used to evaluate the reliability of devices and components that are not repaired.

Mean time between failures (MTBF) is the rating on a device or devices that predicts the expected time between failures. Based on the MTTF and/or MTBF of a system, you must consider and plan for the necessary redundancy measures.

A list of failure points with their redundancy measures are explained below:

Disks

The Redundant Array of Independent Disks (RAID) standards are a set of vendor-independent specifications mostly for fault tolerant configurations on multiple-disk systems. If one or more of the disks fail, data can be recovered from the remaining disks. RAID can be implemented through operating system software, but hardware-based RAID implementations are more efficient and more widely deployed.

There are several RAID levels, each of which provides a combination of features and efficiencies. RAID levels are identified by number; RAID 0, RAID 1 and RAID 5 are the most common. All RAID forms except RAID 0 reduce the threat of loss due to disk failures and provide protection.

Circuits

To reduce the damage caused by the loss of a communications circuit in a data network, a backup circuit should be made available and installed to serve as a redundant connection.

Servers

Server clustering allows servers to work together to provide access, ensuring minimal data loss from a server failure. Should one of the servers in the cluster fail, the remaining servers, or server, will assume the responsibilities, but with the possibility of decreased performance. When the failed server is restored, it will integrate back into the cluster and reinstate with a minimal noticeable shift in performance.

Routers

Router redundancy is the technique of deploying multiple routers in teams to limit the risk of routing failure should a router malfunction. The routers share the same configuration and act as one route and control information. If a redundant router fails, the remaining routers assume the load and sustain the routing process.

General hardware

Periodically add spare parts to your network to test them; in the event of an emergency, they can be the difference between shutting down business and operating at a reduced – but acceptable – level.

Power supplies

A recent feature of power supplies is to include two or more units built into one system with capabilities for each to supply power to the entire system. If one of the unit fails, then by means of a hot swap built into the server, the other unit supplies power.

Network adapters

Systems can also be supplied with built-in redundant network adapters that automatically hot-swap if one fails.

High Availability

High availability is a rating that expresses how closely systems approach the goal of providing data availability 100% of the time while maintaining a high level of system performance. The systems are usually rated as a percentage that shows the proportion of expected uptime to total time. Some of the methods used in achieving this include clustering, load balancing and redundancy measures.

DRP Testing and Maintenance

Every DRP should be tested periodically as part of its implementation and your DRP development process should include an evaluation phase to ensure its effectiveness. The U.S Federal Emergency Management Agency (FEMA) recognizes and recommends several types of exercises that you can use to evaluate DRPs.

Walkthroughs, workshops and orientation seminars

Often used to provide basic awareness and training for disaster recovery team members, these exercises describe the contents of BCPs, DRPs and other plans and the roles and responsibilities outlined in those plans.

Tabletop exercises

Discussion-based sessions where disaster recovery team members discuss their roles in emergency situations, as well as their responses to particular situations.

Functional exercises

Action-based sessions where employees can validate DRPs by performing scenario-based activities in a simulated environment.

Full-scale exercises

Action-based sessions that reflect real situations, these exercises are held onsite and use real equipment and real personnel as much as possible. Full-scale exercises are often conducted by public agencies, but local organizations might be asked to participate.

After the plan has been completed, you should review it at least annually and make any maintenance-level changes required based on the results of the review as well as the results of periodic testing.

Guidelines for Planning a Disaster Recovery

To plan for a disaster recovery, you must properly assess your organization's current state of readiness and you must know when and how to improve any limitations of the current strategy.

- Regularly test the BCP or DRP in offline scenarios that use only backup resources.

- Websites such as www.disasterrecoveryforum.com or www.disasterrecoveryworld.com are sites available for DRP and/or BCP research.

- Ensure redundancy measures are in place for servers, power supplies and your ISP.

- Verify there is access to spare hardware and peripherals for emergency use and that the devices are secure enough to conduct business with.

- Review any service level agreements (SLAs) that are in place so that are in place so that you have an idea of what constitutes acceptable downtime.

- Create a line of communication that does not make use of company resources, so it does not break should the company lose power after hours.

- Identify and document all single points of failure, as well as any up-to-date redundancy measures.

- Make sure that the company's redundant storage is secure.

- Be sure that a DRP includes provisions for regular tests of the plan. You may schedule a "free drill", where all managers are moved to an offsite location, unannounced to help simulate a disaster or emergency, which does not always provide ample warning.

- Employees must receive training to understand the importance of the DRP.

Execute DRPs and Procedures

The Disaster Recovery Process

Notify stakeholders

Stakeholders should be informed of a business-critical disaster. They may consist of senior management, board members, investors, clients, suppliers, employees and the public. Different categories of stakeholders are notified at different times and the level of detail follows the notification procedures in your policy.

Begin emergency operations

The DRP should contain detailed steps regarding specific emergency services. An incident manager should be appointed to assume control of the situation and ensure the safety of personnel.

Assess the damage

A damage assessment should be conducted to determine the extent of incurred facility damages, to identify the cause of the disaster if it is unclear and to estimate the amount of expected downtime. This assessment can also determine the appropriate response strategy.

Assess the facility

It is necessary to assess the current facility's ability to continue being the primary location of operation. If the facility has been adversely affected and has suffered significant losses, relocating to an alternate site may be the best option.

Begin recovery process

Once you have notified stakeholders, performed the initial emergency operations and assessed the damage and the facility's ability to function, then it is time to start the recovery process.

The Recovery Team

The recovery team is a group of designated individuals who implement recovery procedures and control recovery operations in the event of an internal or external disruption to critical business processes. The recovery team immediately responds in an emergency and restores critical business processes to their normal operating capacity, at the remote or recovery site, once key services and information systems are back online.

Secure Recovery

The BCP or DRP must include provisions for securely recovering data, systems and other sensitive resources. This might mean designating a trusted administrator to supervise the recovery, as well as documenting the steps and information needed to restore the processes, systems and data needed to recover from the disaster and instructions for continuing operations either at the primary site or an alternate site. The secure recovery process should be reviewed and tested on a regular basis.

Backup Types and Recovery Plans

There are three main types of backups.

Full backup

All selected files, regardless of the state of the archived bit, are
backed up. The archive bit is a file property that essentially indicates
whether the file has been modified since it was last backed up. A full
backup then clears the archive bit.

Differential backup

All selected files that have changed since the last full backup are
backed up. A differential backup does not clear the archive bit.
When differential backups are used, you must restore the last full
backup plus the most recent differential backup.

Incremental backup

All selected files that have changed since the last full or differential
backup are backed up. It clears the archive bit. An incremental
backup typically takes less time to perform than a differential
backup because it includes less data. When incremental backups are
used, you must restore the last full backup plus all subsequent
incremental backups.

Backout Contingency Plans

A backout contingency plan is a documented plan that includes
specific procedures and processes that are applied in the event that
a change or modification made to a system must be undone. The
plan may include key individuals, a list of systems, backout time
frames and the specific steps needed to fully undo a change. Part of
the plan may also include a backup plan that may be deployed as
part of the backout processes and procedures.

Secure Backups

Backing up sensitive or important data is only part of the solution, as that backup also needs to be secure. Storing copies of sensitive or critical information is a sensible security practice and should not simply be limited to a secondary hard disk or tape archive. A backup can be considered most secure if it is offline and offsite and stored in an environment that is physically locked and protected from environmental intrusions such as fire or water.

Backup Storage Locations

The magnetic tapes or other physical media used to create data backups must be stored securely but must remain accessible in case the data is needed. Many organizations employ both onsite and offsite backup storage. The onsite storage location is for the most recent set of backups, so that they can be accessed quickly if a data restoration is needed during normal operations. The offsite location is a secure, disaster-resistant storage facility where the organization keeps either a duplicate or an older backup set to protect it against any damage caused by disaster conditions at the primary site.

Guidelines for Executing DRPs and Procedures

- The organization needs to identify the team that will handle the disaster situation, including the incident manager.

- Each disaster recovery team member must have clearly laid out roles and responsibilities and must be easily accessible to the other employees.

- Employees must be aware of the members of the disaster recovery team and must know who they need to contact in the event of a disaster.

- Inform stakeholders as specified in your DRP.

- Roll out emergency services, such as an alternate site, under the control of the incident manager.

- The damage to the main site should be assessed and the recovery team should be brought in to repair any physical damage and assess the extent to which the main site can be restored.

- A restoration of the backup should be done of all files that have been compromised or deleted.

- Decisions should be made to purchase or replace missing system elements.

- Once the recovery process is completed, document the steps taken and save a report to be used in case of another recovery process.